Escape Your Routine and Visit the Most Popular West Coast National Parks

Popular West Coast National Parks

Tony George Glez

Table of Contents

Introduction

Are you tired of the chaotic life in the city and wish to find an escape? National parks can be your answer. In the United States, there are currently 63 national parks spread across the entire country. If you want to begin exploring the beauty of nature, consider visiting one of these national parks. Every one of them has its own unique charm and appeal that draws large numbers of tourists each year, nationally and internationally. National parks are among the most beautiful destinations in the country, especially for those who enjoy photography. However, many people have yet to learn how great these parks are, and that's why it's worth making the trip.

National parks are an amazing idea for everyone because they're known to be fairly cheap to enter, which makes them budget-friendly. Because they're spread across 27 different states, it's very easy to access them as well. If you have kids, national parks can provide them a space to learn about nature, history, and conservation while also enjoying fun activities. Moreover, spending time in nature also improves your overall well-being because you can step back from your phones and computers. This means that you'll have more time to do outside activities like hiking or walking, which will boost your physical health. It's time for you to relax and visit a national park!

Which national park will you visit first? If you need help figuring out where to begin, I'll provide you with information about the most popular and stunning West Coast national parks in this book. What are they?

- Yellowstone National Park

- Grand Teton National Park

- Yosemite National Park

- Grand Canyon National Park

- Mount Rainier National Park

- Rocky Mountain National Park

This book will give you insights into the history and culture of these national parks as well as their operating hours and seasons. You'll be provided with basic yet essential information like fees and passes, interagency passes, permits, maps, and camping. There will be tips and fun activities that you can consider doing during your visit. Not only that, but you'll also discover their best hiking trails and safety measures. This means you don't have to worry about how to start your preparation because all the information you need is here. This book may also be a great guide when you're about to plan your visit.

You might ask why you should be listening to me right now. Well, I've always been passionate about sports and the outdoors. In my free time, I often choose to explore nature by hiking, camping, or just taking a stroll with my pet. After years of doing this, I realized that spending time in nature has so many physical and mental advantages. Through this book, I want to invite all of you to start traveling to these national parks to experience the benefits first-hand. Who knows, you might get addicted and become passionate about these outdoor activities like me. If you're tired of the city, it's time to get off your couch and pack up your bag for an adventure!

Are you ready to learn how to prepare to visit West Coast national parks? Let's explore them one by one.

Chapter 1:

Yellowstone National Park

As you begin planning your next vacation destination, you should consider visiting Yellowstone National Park because it's one of the most popular ones on the West Coast. Did you know Yellowstone is the first and oldest national park in the United States? It was established in 1872 (Dierickx, 2015). Additionally, the Yellowstone Caldera located there is a volcano that caused three of the six largest volcanic eruptions in recorded history. Do these facts make you excited to visit Yellowstone?

History and Culture

Yellowstone National Park is spanned across three different states, including Montana, Wyoming, and Idaho. This means the park has a vast area that's perfect for those who enjoy exploring nature because you'll never run out of things to see. As for its geographical location, the park is where the Columbia Plateau, Great Plains, and Great Basin all meet (*Yellowstone at 150 years*, 2022). Moreover, the park got its name from the yellow sandstones discovered in the Yellowstone River located in Montana.

Since it was founded in 1872, Yellowstone National Park has been operating for over 150 years. However, humans have inhabited the area for over 10,000 years—long before the national park was established. This makes it filled with complex human and natural histories that are still developing to this day. Before the European colonies came to the US, Yellowstone was utilized by different Native American tribes as a place to build their homes, hunt animals, collect food, and travel through. These tribes took advantage of the land while also preserving its culture and resources. In total, there are 27 tribes that have ties to the park, and some of them are the Cheyenne River Sioux, Crow Creek Sioux, Colville Reservation, and Salish and Kootenai (*Yellowstone at 150 years*, 2022).

What is Yellowstone known for? We've all heard about the Grand Canyon in Yellowstone; it's one of the most popular destinations there. It attracts a lot of tourists because of its hiking trails. It covers an area of over 20 miles within the park. There are also some lookout points that you may choose to drive along or hike to enjoy the beautiful scenery. Many people are also drawn to the canyon because of the geographical details, like its rock structures and colors. Some say that it's best to visit the canyon early in the morning to see the sunrise or late in the day to watch the sunset.

Another known destination in Yellowstone is Old Faithful. The geyser is undoubtedly breathtaking to watch because its eruptions can extend up to 180 feet in the air. The eruptions have happened once every 90 minutes since 2019, and they may last for a few minutes (Parker, 2023b). However, you must check with the information center in order to know the exact time of these eruptions. Around the area, you'll also be able to find hotels, restaurants, and parking lots, so you won't have to worry about rushing, and you can really enjoy your time there.

Since Yellowstone covers a lot of land, there are large numbers of animals inhabiting the park. It's also said that this park has one of the most diverse animal populations in the United States. How many species reside in Yellowstone? Well, right now, there are over 300 animal species living there (Croft, 2022). You'll encounter these animals when you go hiking or driving in the park. Additionally, some common animals you may find easily when visiting include bison, rabbits, and elk. However, there are also a few predator species that you need to watch out for, such as coyotes, cougars, and grizzly bears. Make sure you know what these predators look like so that you can stay away from them.

Basic Information

In this section, I'll provide essential information you need to know before visiting Yellowstone. Let's explore more about these things, from its operating hours and seasons to the camping grounds available in the park.

Operating Seasons and Hours

Before you visit Yellowstone National Park, you have to ensure it's open. Imagine going there and finding out that the destination you want to visit is closed—that would be a waste of time. The park is open all year, but there is restricted access during spring, winter, and fall. Regardless of what day it is, Yellowstone can be entered 24/7 through the northern entrance of the park. During fall, some roads will start to be restricted. Throughout the winter season, there will be snow coach and snowmobiling tours, which restrict access to interior destinations like the Old Faithful Geyser and Grand Canyon. Many facilities inside are also closed during winter because the roads can't be accessed. When spring comes, the roads will start to open to vehicles. In the summer, all roads are open again. However, there might be some construction that delays you.

Furthermore, operating hours rely on the visitor center. Here are the opening hours of some visitor centers:

- **Canyon Visitor Education Center:** 8 a.m. to 6 p.m.

- **Albright Visitor Center:** 9 a.m. to 6 p.m.

- **West Yellowstone Visitor Information Center:** 8 a.m. to 8 p.m.

- **West Thumb Information Station:** 9 a.m. to 5 p.m.

- **Old Faithful Visitor Education Center:** 8 a.m. to 8 p.m.

- **Fishing Bridge Visitor Center and Trailside Museum:** 8 a.m. to 6 p.m.

- **Madison Information Station:** 9 a.m. to 4:30 p.m.

- **Grant Visitor Center:** 8 a.m. to 6 p.m.

- **Norris Geyser Basin Museum and Information Center:** 9 a.m. to 6 p.m.

- **Museum of the National Park Ranger:** 10 a.m. to 4 p.m.

These are the normal opening hours of the visitor centers. You must check for holidays, seasonal exceptions, and closures before visiting. You may check the accurate information on the *NPS Yellowstone* app. To avoid visiting when there's a closure, you need to check it often because the schedule might change from time to time.

Fees and Passes

Prior to entering Yellowstone, you must purchase a pass at the entrance. You have two choices for a pass: a seven-day pass or an annual entrance (Holden, 2021). If you intend to go to the park several times a year, buying the yearly pass is cheaper than the seven-day entrance. The following are the prices of the park passes:

- **Standard entrance for seven days:** $2o–$35

- **Annual entrance pass:** $70

Interagency Passes

Interagency passes are also called the America the Beautiful National Parks Pass Series because they can get you to different federal sites all over the US like Acadia and Grand Teton National Parks (*Places to get interagency passes*, 2023). These interagency passes have different requirements and purposes. Most of these passes need authentic documentation in order for you to be eligible for them. There are seven of these passes; here are the details:

1. **Senior Pass:** This one is made for people who are considered seniors, who are people over 62 years old. This is only available for those with US citizenship and permanent residency. The prices are $80 for a lifetime entrance and $20 for an annual one.

2. **Volunteer Pass:** This entrance pass is free of charge. However, you need to complete 250 hours of volunteer work at a federal organization. You may ask your organization if you can apply for this entrance pass.

3. **Annual Pass:** This one is available for everybody who wishes to have a yearly entrance for this interagency pass, it costs $80.

4. **Access Pass:** It's provided for those with US citizenship and permanent residency who have lifelong disabilities. This is also free of charge and can be used for lifetime access.

5. **Military Annual Pass:** This is made for US military personnel, and it's free of charge. To get this pass, you must bring evidence that you're currently an active member of the military.

6. **Fourth Grade Pass:** It's a free entrance pass for children in 4th grade, including during summer break. However, they must provide documentation that proves they're currently in the 4th grade.

7. **Military Lifetime Pass:** This one is a free pass created for military veterans of the United States. You must provide a valid veteran ID to be eligible for this pass.

Permits

Just like interagency passes, permits also have a particular or special purpose. Permits are made for those who wish to hold certain activities or events in the park. A permit is necessary so that the National Park Service can oversee and control the activity to protect the public and resources within the park. Some events that will need a permit are wedding ceremonies, filming, and photography activities.

Accommodations

Perhaps you wish to visit Yellowstone to learn its history, explore nature, go hiking, or relax from your chaotic life. Whatever your reason is, you'll need to choose the right place to stay. There are many lodging and accommodation options to choose from if you plan to stay the night in the park, as follows:

- **Lake Yellowstone Hotel:** This is the oldest hotel within Yellowstone National Park since it was opened in 1891 (Peglar, 2021b). With its classic style, this hotel radiates elegance.

- **Old Faithful Inn:** If you enjoy learning about history, this one is a great option for you. This inn is considered a historic landmark located within the park that has stood for almost 120 years because it was built in 1904 (Peglar, 2022b). When you enter it, you'll feel like going back in time because of its rustic style. It was built from logs and stones that were sourced locally.

- **Mammoth Hot Springs Hotel and Cabins:** This property was named because it's located close to hot springs with the same name. It was established in 1936, even though the building itself was built in 1911 (Mishev, 2023). In this hotel, you may even have the chance to see elk around the property.

- **Roosevelt Lodge:** This lodge was made with just 80 cabins and was built in 1920 (Mishev, 2023). Just like the Old Faithful Inn, it also has a rustic style. Moreover, you're provided with rocking chairs on the terrace where you can relax and unwind your thoughts.

- **Canyon Lodge:** This lodge is located within Yellowstone and is considered the biggest accommodation because it has 500 rooms (Peglar, 2022c). It went through extensive renovation for over a year and became the most sustainable and eco-friendly lodging in the park.

The most popular hotels are Old Faithful Inn and Canyon Lodge, which are always fully booked all year long. If you can't manage to find a room in one of these hotels, you may also search for one on the western side of Yellowstone in Montana.

Campgrounds

Within Yellowstone, there are 12 different campgrounds provided for those who wish to camp outside. If you want to stay at one of these campgrounds, you must reserve it before visiting. Since there are large numbers of visitors each year, I recommend that you book the campsite as soon as you can. Here's a list of campgrounds to consider:

Name	Price (Nightly)
Lewis Lake	$20
Bridge Bay	$33 before taxes
Indian Creek	$20
Canyon	$39 before taxes
Mammoth	$25
Fishing Bridge RV Park	$89 or $99 before taxes
Norris	Not applicable

Grant Village	$39 before taxes
Slough Creek	$20
Madison	$33 before taxes
Tower Fall	Not applicable
Pebble Creek	$20

These are the campgrounds that are provided in Yellowstone, but Pebble Creek, Mammoth, Norris, and Tower Fall are currently unavailable to the public. Five of the park's campgrounds are run by the lodges that are situated there (Bridge Bay, Fishing Bridge RV Park, Madison, Canyon, and Grant Village). Through the lodges' websites, reservations can be made directly to book the campsite. The rest of them are under the NPS management, and you can reserve them through recreation.gov.

You might be confused and overwhelmed about which one to choose out of these 12 campgrounds. If you wish to stay the night close to the famous Grand Canyon and Old Faithful, there are two perfect campgrounds for you: The first one is Madison because it's located in close proximity to Old Faithful. It's also a great place for those who enjoy fishing because Madison River Flyfishing is nearby. Another one is Canyon because it's situated close to the Grand Canyon. People who love hiking flock to this campground since it's also located near Mount Washburn and Hayden Valley.

Tips for Camping in Yellowstone

Before visiting Yellowstone, you must plan your trip ahead of time. If you plan to camp within the park, here are a few tips to make your planning easier when choosing a great campsite:

- You should book a campsite in advance. It's true that Yellowstone has 12 campgrounds, but it may still be difficult to get one if you want to visit during summer. This is why it's important to reserve your chosen campground online first. Most of the time, the campgrounds are fully booked during the holidays and weekends.

- To make your trip efficient, you need to reserve a campsite close to the destinations you want to visit. Yellowstone National Park is not a small area, so it's essential to stay at a place that has easier access to what you're most excited to see. For example, if you wish to visit the Grand Canyon, you may reserve a campsite at Canyon Campground.

- You need to also prepare yourself for cold weather during the night, even in the summer months. Since every campground in Yellowstone is over 6,000 feet above sea level, the temperature there can be cold all year long (Maxwell, 2020). If you camp in a tent, you must make sure to bring thick blankets and gloves to keep yourself warm.

- I've mentioned before that there are different predators in Yellowstone, like grizzly bears. This is why you have to follow safety measures when camping in the park. For instance, you must store your food properly to avoid attracting unwanted predators to your campsite. After eating, you need to check if there are food scraps lying around and put them in a container. This will protect you and help keep the park clean.

- If you plan your trip using an RV, you must check if the length doesn't exceed the limit. Most campgrounds don't have space for an RV that's longer than 30 feet, so you must be aware of the limitations and maximum lengths before you reserve a campsite (Jones, 2023a).

- If you wish to take your pet with you, you must know that you won't be able to bring them on the hiking trails. But you also can't leave them alone at the campsite, which means that you need to have someone always keeping a watch on them when you're going somewhere.

Fun Activities to Do

When organizing your Yellowstone itinerary, you'll want to include different fun activities to do. There are actually so many different things you can do in the park during the winter or summer months. If you're confused about what to choose, I'll give you a few options to consider.

Winter

During the winter, Yellowstone receives so much snow each year. Because of this, most roads and facilities within the park are closed to the public. However, this doesn't mean that you can't visit. Actually, it becomes more of an adventure because there are some winter activities you can do.

Skiing and Snowshoeing

Because the park is covered with snow in the winter, it becomes a perfect place to ski and snowshoe. In fact, there are various trails to explore for those who enjoy these activities. However, they're not the safest activities you can do out there, which means that you must take precautions beforehand. The following are essential tips and safety measures for skiing and snowshoeing:

- **Creating a flexible plan:** During winter, you don't know how the weather will change. This means that you must make considerations for daylight limitations, harsh temperatures, and snowfall.

- **Speaking to park rangers:** Before skiing and snowshoeing, you must ask park rangers to get accurate information, like unavailable trails.

- **Wearing proper clothing:** Because the weather in winter can be extreme, you must layer your clothing and wear thick gloves as well as socks to avoid getting hypothermia and frostbite.

- **Drinking enough water:** The climate during winter can be cold and dry, so it might cause dehydration. It's crucial to drink enough water beforehand and also bring some water with you. A Thermos bottle will be helpful to keep it from freezing.

- **Avoiding wildlife:** When you see wild animals, you must stop and let them pass first. You also need to stay away from big animals like bison, and never show yourself in front of predators, such as wolves.

- **Having someone with you:** When skiing and snowshoeing, you need to always bring somebody. You must inform them what trail you take, where you're going, and what time you'll finish.

Winter Backcountry Camping

Another activity you may consider is backcountry camping in the park. Unlike camping at a normal campsite, you'll stay at a place where there are no roads or developed areas. This means that it's a more challenging experience and definitely not for the weak. You must get a permit for backcountry camping a few days before you go.

Furthermore, you must also pack essential items for backcountry camping. You need to bring a tent and a sleeping bag to serve as shelter. To melt snow and get fresh water, you might want to bring a cooking pot. To be ready for extreme weather, you should pack additional clothing like gloves, hats, and socks. You must also bring extra food for a day or two in case something delays your trip back. To know the direction you're going, it's also essential to have a map or a compass. These are just some basic things, and you may bring other items according to your needs.

There are also rules you must follow, and here are some of them:

- Lighting a fire is not permitted.

- All trash must be cleaned and packed from the area.

- Bringing a pet is not allowed.

- Feeding wild animals is forbidden.

- Staying more than three nights at a location is not allowed.

- The limit of a group is only 12 people.

Not only that, but there are also several travel considerations you have to keep in mind because backcountry camping is a risky activity. What are some of these considerations?

- You must inform someone where you plan to go and when you're coming back.

- You can't depend on your phone to communicate, so you need to prepare for an emergency.

- You need to make sure that your tent has good ventilation to avoid the build-up of carbon monoxide that may cause poisoning.

- Extreme weather during winter is dangerous and may cause death, so you must wear proper clothing at all times.

Riding a Snowcoach and Snowmobile

Because the roads are closed during the winter, you won't be able to use your own vehicle to enter the park. The best method to go sightseeing within Yellowstone is by taking a snowcoach or snowmobile tour. This way, you may still visit the Grand Canyon and Old Faithful even in the winter months. A snowcoach is a vehicle where you can ride with other people, while a snowmobile is one that you may ride yourself. No matter what you choose, there'll be a tour guide to lead the way.

Summer

Although there are some fun activities during the winter, it's still very limited compared to the summer months. As the weather gets warmer, the roads, lodges, and attractions start to open again for visitors. This is also the perfect season to see animals like elk and bison graze on the green field. Not only that, but there are also many more activities to choose from if you plan to visit. What are these fun activities?

Visiting Thermal Basins

In Yellowstone, there are many thermal basins, such as geysers and hot springs. The best time to visit them is during the summer months. It's said that more than 50% of the active geysers in the world are located in the park (Snell, 2022). The most known ones are the Old Faithful Geyser and the Grand Prismatic Spring. However, these thermal basins may change dramatically over time, so it doesn't get boring if you keep revisiting them. How do they work? Water from the ground receives heat from a volcano, which is then brought up to the earth's surface, creating a thermal basin (*Explore thermal basins*, 2023).

Before visiting one of them, there are several safety precautions you must know first:

- You must always stick to established pathways, and hold your kids' hands to prevent them from running off.

- You're not allowed to throw things into the thermal basins.

- You should never enter or swim in the hot springs because the water may burn your skin.

- If you start to feel queasy, leave the vicinity right away because you may be affected by toxic gasses.

Hiking a Trail

You might want to drive around the park, but it can't beat hiking if you want to enjoy the scenery to its fullest. In Yellowstone, there are a lot of different hiking trails to choose whether you're a beginner or an expert. Before we explore all the hiking trails in Yellowstone, here are some safety tips first:

- You must dress properly. To make sure you enjoy the hiking experience, you should dress according to the season of your visit. You might want to only wear a tank top and short pants during the hike, but that will not protect your body from bugs or insects. It's much better to wear long sleeves.

- You should never go beyond the trails. The park has so many dangerous things like wild animals and thermal basins. By staying on the trail, you'll avoid getting into dangerous situations.

- You need to bring enough drinking water. Hiking can be a tiring experience, so you have to make sure to stay hydrated.

- You should bring a map, GPS, or compass to avoid getting lost.

- You should also keep bug and bear spray with you at all times.

- You should avoid hiking alone and always go with other people to avoid unwanted accidents.

- You may also bring sunglasses and sunscreen to protect your eyes and body from the sun.

So, what are the hiking trails available in Yellowstone?

Canyon Day Hikes

Trail	Description
Seven Mile Hole	Distance/Duration: 2.3 miles/5–8 hours Difficulty: Hard (hot springs along

	the way)
Observation Peak	Distance/Duration: 2.6 miles/5–6 hours Difficulty: Hard (not for those who have respiratory or heart issues)
Mount Washburn Spur	Distance/Duration: 11.1 miles/8–10 hours Difficulty: Hard (not advised for those who have respiratory or heart issues)
Ribbon Lake	Distance/Duration: 2.3 miles/3–4 hours Difficulty: Moderate
Howard Eaton at the Canyon Area	Distance/Duration: 13.4 miles/5–6 hours Difficulty: Moderate (can be slippery and muddy during the rainy season)
Dunraven Pass—Mount Washburn	Distance/Duration: 4.5 miles/3–6 hours Difficulty: Hard (not good for those who have respiratory or heart issues)

Cascade Lake	Distance/Duration: 1.25 miles/2–3 hours Difficulty: Easy
Grebe Lake	Distance/Duration: 3.5 miles/3–4 hours Difficulty: Easy
Chittenden Road—Mount Washburn	Distance/Duration: 5.6 miles/3–5 hours Difficulty: Hard (not for those who have respiratory or heart issues)

Lake and Fishing Bridge Day Hikes

Trail	Description
Elephant Back Mountain	Distance/Duration: 1.25 miles/2–3 hours Difficulty: Easy
Avalanche Peak	Distance/Duration: 2.1 miles/3–4 hours Difficulty: Hard (not for those who have respiratory or heart issues)

Natural Bridge	Distance/Duration: 3.1 miles/1–2 hours Difficulty: Moderate (watch out for slippery and wet rocks)
Mud Volcano	Distance/Duration: 0.8 mile/1–2 hours Difficulty: Easy
Pelican Valley	Distance/Duration: 6.2 miles/3–4 hours Difficulty: Easy
Pelican Creek Nature	Distance/Duration: 1 mile/30–60 minutes Difficulty: Easy
Storm Point	Distance/Duration: 3 miles/ 1–2 hours Difficulty: Easy

Madison Day Hikes

Trail	Description
Purple Mountain	Distance/Duration: 3 miles/3–5 hours Difficulty: Hard (challenging hike

	and not for those with heart or respiratory conditions)
Harlequin Lake	Distance/Duration: 1 mile/30–60 minutes Difficulty: Easy

Mammoth Hot Springs Day Hikes

Trail	Description
Wraith Falls	Distance/Duration: 0.5 mile/30–60 minutes Difficulty: Easy
Sepulcher Mountain	Distance/Duration: 11.2 miles/6–8 hours Difficulty: Hard (grizzly bears are often seen on this trail)
Beaver Ponds	Distance/Duration: 5.5 miles/2–5 hours Difficulty: Moderate (the trail has 350 feet elevation)
Blacktail Deer Creek to Yellowstone River	Distance/Duration: 8.2 miles/4–5 hours Difficulty: Easy

Rescue Creek	Distance/Duration: 8 miles/4–6 hours Difficulty: Moderate
Osprey Falls	Distance/Duration: 9.8 miles/4–6 hours Difficulty: Hard
Lava Creek	Distance/Duration: 8.6 miles/2–3 hours Difficulty: Moderate
Bunsen Peak	Distance/Duration: 4.4 miles/2–3 hours Difficulty: Moderate (grizzly bears often pass through this trail)
Mammoth Hot Springs Trails	Distance/Duration: 30–90 minutes Difficulty: Moderate

Old Faithful Day Hikes

Trail	Description
Observation Point	Distance/Duration: 7 miles/1–3 hours

	Difficulty: Moderate
Mystic Falls	Distance/Duration: 3.5 miles/2–4 hours Difficulty: Moderate
Howard Eaton at the Old Faithful Area	Distance/Duration: 13.4 miles/3–5 hours Difficulty: Moderate (bear activity is often seen here)
Fairy Falls	Distance/Duration: 4.8 miles/3–5 hours Difficulty: Easy
Mallard Lake	Distance/Duration: 7.3 miles/3–6 hours Difficulty: Moderate (bear activity can be seen here)
Lone Star Geyser	Distance/Duration: 5.3 miles/2–3 hours Difficulty: Easy
Grand Prismatic Overlook	Distance/Duration: 1.5 miles/1–2 hours Difficulty: Easy

Sentinel Meadows and Queen's Laundry	Distance/Duration: 5.1 miles/2–4 hours Difficulty: Moderate

Tower and Northeast Day Hikes

Trail	Description
Yellowstone River Picnic Area	Distance/Duration: 3.9 miles/2–3 hours Difficulty: Easy
Trout Lake	Distance/Duration: 1.2 miles/1–2 hours Difficulty: Easy
Hellroaring	Distance/Duration: 2.1 miles/3–5 hours Difficulty: Moderate (it's a backcountry trail)
Garnet Hill	Distance/Duration: 9.8 miles/4–5 hours Difficulty: Moderate (bears and bison often pass through here)
Specimen Ridge Day Hike	Distance/Duration: 16.9 miles/2–4 hours

	Difficulty: Hard (it has a high-elevation path and is not for anyone with heart or respiratory issues)
Slough Creek	Distance/Duration: 19.8 miles/2–5 hours Difficulty: Hard
Lost Lake	Distance/Duration: 3 miles/1–2 hours Difficulty: Moderate

West Thumb and Grant Day Hikes

Trail	Description
Lewis River Channel or Dogshead	Distance/Duration: 11 miles/5–8 hours Difficulty: Moderate (it's a backcountry trail)
Duck Lake	Distance/Duration: 0.9 mile/1–2 hours Difficulty: Moderate
Yellowstone Lake Overlook	Distance/Duration: 1.7 miles/1–3 hours Difficulty: Moderate (thermal

	activity throughout the trail)
West Thumb Geyser Basin	Distance/Duration: 1 mile/30–60 minutes Difficulty: Easy
DeLacy Creek	Distance/Duration: 6.3 miles/3–5 hours Difficulty: Easy
Riddle Lake	Distance/Duration: 4.7 miles/2–4 hours Difficulty: Easy

Viewing Wildlife

I've mentioned before that Yellowstone is a park with diverse animal populations. If you enjoy learning about animals, the park is one of the best destinations to watch wildlife. There are also various tours available, and you can choose based on what animals you'd like to see. For example, you may find moose and elk in the West Thumb area or bison, mule deer, black bears, and wolves in Lamar Valley (*Watch wildlife*, 2021). However, we all know that wild animals can be dangerous, so it's important to take safety precautions when watching them. The following are several safety tips you need to know:

- You shouldn't get too close or approach any animals because you might get attacked or injured.

- You should never feed the animals because the food can be harmful to their bodies.

- When watching wildlife, you should go on a tour because you might not know how to protect yourself from predators if you go alone.

- If you see an animal approaching you, you must step away quietly or hide at a safe distance.

- When watching bears, you must always stay in your car to avoid getting attacked.

Biking Around Yellowstone

If you don't want to drive or hike in the park, biking can be a good option. Although it's lovely to drive around Yellowstone, biking is even better because you'll get to take your time and relax while enjoying the beautiful scenery around you. Most areas in Yellowstone are open for those who want to bike, and there are also bike trails available. Yellowstone allows road bikes, mountain bikes, and electric bikes to be used on paved public roads as well as parking lots and bike trails (*Biking*, 2023). However, it's also crucial to do it safely, here are a few tips:

- You should wear a strong helmet to protect your head in case you fall off the bike.

- You have to bring sunscreen when biking in the summer to protect your face and body from the sun.

- You need to bring water and food as well as additional clothing.

- Prior to crossing a road, you must slow down and communicate with the other vehicles by making eye contact and using hand signals.

- You must bring a repair kit in case your bike breaks down.

Horseback Riding

Just like biking, riding a horse in Yellowstone is also a great way to slow down while enjoying the view. Horseback riding can be a unique activity, and if you want this experience, the park offers guided tours around Yellowstone that last for an hour or two. However, if you don't want to ride with other people, you may also take a private trip. The fees for both of these trips will differ, so make sure to check them out ahead of time.

Fishing and Boating

These two activities are very popular with Yellowstone's visitors because there are many great lakes and rivers to choose from. Fishing is popular because there are many fish species inhabiting the lakes and rivers in the park. Boating is also famous since the scenery is beautiful. However, before you go fishing and boating, you must check the date and time to see if they're open. Following that, a permit is essential to acquire. Moreover, you should be prepared for the trip by bringing mosquito repellent, sunscreen, hats, raincoats, drinking water, and other necessary supplies.

Key Takeaways

- Yellowstone National Park was created in 1872 and is situated within Montana, Wyoming, and Idaho states.

- Its complex human history dates back to over 10,000 years ago.

- The most famous and popular attractions in the park are the Old Faithful and Grand Canyon.

- Before visiting, it's important to know some essential information like its operating seasons and hours, fees and passes, interagency passes, permits, lodging and accommodations, and camping.

- In the winter months, some fun activities you can do are skiing and snowshoeing, winter backcountry camping, and riding a snowcoach or snowmobile.

- During the summer, there are more activities like visiting thermal basins, hiking, viewing wildlife, bicycling, horseback riding, fishing, and boating.

In Chapter 2, we'll discuss Grand Teton National Park, including its history and culture, basic information, hiking and camping, and fun activities to do when traveling solo or in groups.

Grand Teton National Park

Have you ever wondered how this national park got its name? The origin of the term "Teton" is one of the most intriguing Grand Teton National Park facts. The Tetons are the stunning and incredible mountain range in the park. The name "Teton" actually has no sexual overtones, although it takes its name from the French word "tétons," which translates to "breasts" in English (Onion et al., 2019). This is because the park was named by French explorers who had a creative imagination and were motivated by the mountain range's shape as they were surveying and mapping the region. In fact, the first world explorers frequently named geographical locations based on various elements, including shape, landscape characteristics, and occasionally their own recollections and memories.

History and Culture

Grand Teton National Park lies in the state of Wyoming and was founded in 1929 (Fink, 2022). This park includes the Teton Range as well as the Jackson Hole Valley (Hein, 2014). For over 11,000 years, these areas have been inhabited by humans because many were drawn by their breathtaking beauty and diverse animal and plant species.

When Europeans first discovered the region, there were already some Native American tribes residing there. Some of these tribes were Flathead, Blackfoot, Shoshone, and Crow (Hein, 2014). These tribes visited the area mostly during the summer months because there was plenty of food to gather and animals to hunt. As the cold winter drew near, they would leave for a warmer region. In the beginning, the Europeans who visited were explorers and fur trappers before those who wished to gain wealth and settle. When people began settling in the Jackson Hole region, the cowboy lifestyle started to become popular (Fink, 2022).

What are the most iconic destinations in Grand Teton? There are several big lakes within the park, but the most known one is Jenny Lake. This lake is famous for its mirror-like reflection of the mountain range and is considered the best place for those who wish to view Jackson Hole (Julie, 2023b). You may also drive along the road to see the amazing view of this lake. If you don't wish to drive or walk, you can go kayaking or canoeing to enjoy the scenery better. This will also give you some quiet time instead of joining the crowd by driving or walking.

Grand Teton is also where Inspiration Point and Hidden Falls are located. Inspiration Point is a destination to go to if you want to look over Jenny Lake, and Hidden Falls is a waterfall close to it. Most people who visit the park will go to both of them because of the short distance between the two. They're the perfect destination if you enjoy a small hiking trail since it's only 2.4 miles (Julie, 2023b). However, if you don't like hiking, you can also reach them by boat.

Another known attraction at the park is the Mormon Row. This is considered a historic district established by some Mormon families in the 1890s (Jones, 2023c). However, the settlement was abandoned long ago and has become a tourist attraction in the park. The Teton Range can be seen from this property, which makes it a popular destination for photographers.

Furthermore, there are many unique animals that inhabit the park because of its deep forests and large mountains. Black and grizzly bears are some known wildlife that can be discovered there because of the grassy meadows. Not only that, but you'll also find moose, elk, and bison grazing on the fields and in the wooded areas. Of course, there are also other smaller animals, such as coyotes, beavers, and insects, all over the park. With its diverse animal populations, Grand Teton has become a great destination for watching wildlife in its natural habitat.

Basic Information

Before visiting Grand Teton, you must know some basic information to navigate your trip better. In this part, I'll inform you of the essentials that you need to keep in mind. I'll include the operating hours and seasons, fees and passes, permits, and more.

Operating Seasons and Hours

No matter what season it is, Grand Teton National Park opens its gate 24/7. However, most visitors would choose the summer months to get the best experience, which is May through September. This is because everything is open to the public, such as all of the roads, lodges, and facilities. In the winter, the park will close most of its roads and facilities, so you won't be able to enjoy the park to the fullest.

Additionally, operating hours will rely on the visitor center you go to. The list of the visitor centers is as follows:

- **Laurence S. Rockefeller Preserve Center:** 8 a.m. to 6 p.m.

- **Jenny Lake Ranger Station:** 8 a.m. to 5 p.m.

- **Jenny Lake Visitor Center:** 8 a.m. to 5 p.m.

- **Flag Ranch Information Station:** 9 a.m. to 3:30 p.m.

- **Craig Thomas Discovery and Visitor Center:** 8 a.m. to 7 p.m.

- **Colter Bay Visitor Center:** 8 a.m. to 5 p.m.

These are the normal operating hours of the visitor centers. Before going there, you should make sure to check for any updated information since there might be holidays, seasonal exceptions, and closures at Grand Teton.

Fees and Passes

Before entering Grand Teton, you'll have to pay an entrance fee to get a park pass. When entering the park, you can purchase one of two types of passes: a standard entrance pass is priced at $20 to $35, while an annual pass costs $70. As you might have noticed, the prices are the same as Yellowstone National Park. If you plan to enter the park many times within a year, it's much better to pay for the annual pass to save some money.

Permits

If you plan to do a recreational or special activity at Grand Teton, you must apply for a permit first. Without a permit, you'll be prohibited from doing any of your special celebrations. What are some activities that will require one?

- boating and floating

- climbing

- photography and filming

- wedding parties

- scattering of ashes

- exhibitions

If your activity falls into one of these events, you need to send an email to grte_visitor_service@nps.gov after completing the Special Event Application Form (*Grand Teton permits and reservations*, 2023). This must be done about a month before the scheduled day.

Accommodations

Since Grand Teton is a big national park, you may want to explore for a couple of days and stay the night nearby. Therefore, you must select lodging that best meets your needs. In this section, I'll provide you with the best lodging options to consider, as follows:

- **Colter Bay Cabins:** Situated close to Jackson Lake, this lodging option is available from the end of May to September. It's considered a budget-friendly accommodation with various log and tent cabins to choose from. There's also a horseback riding activity near the property.

- **Headwaters Lodge and Cabins at Flagg Ranch:** This one is open from June to September. It's also a log-style property that has a rustic touch to it. Additionally, you can choose to stay in a hotel room and camper cabin at this lodge. Close to the accommodation, you may do some activities like fishing and floating.

- **Jenny Lake Lodge:** This is a more expensive as well as luxurious option. Moreover, it is available for reservation from June to October. It also has a rustic style and offers privacy since the cabins are surrounded by trees. Just like the name, this lodge is located near Jenny Lake.

- **American Alpine Club Grand Teton Climbers' Ranch:** This option is an affordable place for those who don't have a big budget. It offers log cabins with bunk beds, but you need to bring your own sleeping bag. Some other facilities provided are a shared kitchen and library.

- **Triangle X Ranch:** It's available to reserve from May to October. This one is unique because it has a dude ranch style with a rustic touch (Jones, 2023b). In this accommodation, you can experience Western-style cooking, horseback riding, and fishing.

- **Signal Mountain Lodge:** It opens its doors from May to October. It is a lodge situated right beside Jackson Lake and has log-style cabins. Since it's close to a lake, a few activities to do are canoeing, boating, fishing, and floating.

- **Jackson Lake Lodge:** This is another famous and stunning accommodation within the park because it has breathtaking scenery of the Teton Range (Jones, 2023b). Around this lodge, you can also ride a horse and fish in the lake.

Campgrounds

If you don't want to stay at lodges when visiting Grand Teton, camping can be a great choice for you. By camping, you may better experience the beauty of the park and explore nature. If you've decided to camp, there are several alternatives to this. If you're courageous enough, you may apply for a permit to do backcountry camping. If you want to be more comfortable, you can just rent a campsite to set up your tent or park your RV. Whatever option you choose, you must find out all the things that you need to prepare.

Grand Teton National Park offers eight different campgrounds with over 1,000 campsites available to reserve (*Camping*, 2022). To be able to stay at one of the campgrounds, you must make a reservation. This reservation can be made via Recreation.gov. Camping is very popular at the park, so make sure to reserve a campsite at least six months before your visit. However, if you can't reserve a campsite because everything's fully booked, you may search around the local areas for a private campground. You must know that it's not allowed to camp in the parking lots or on the side of the road. Moreover, the majority of these campgrounds have basic conveniences, such as tables for picnics, flush toilets, tap water, and dump stations.

I'll let you know the current prices of the campgrounds, but you must check them online before visiting in case there's an update. The following is a list of the eight campgrounds along with their prices:

Name	Price (Nightly)
Jenny Lake Campground	$26
Gros Ventre Campground	$26
Colter Bay Campground	$26
Signal Mountain Campground	$31–$50
Colter Bay Tent Village	$26
Colter Bay RV Park	$26
Headwaters Campground	$37.50–$73
Lizard Creek Campground	$29

You might be overwhelmed about which one to choose out of these eight campgrounds. It's best to stay near the destination you really want to visit. For instance, if your main destination is Jenny Lake, you should stay at Jenny Lake Campground. However, if you wish for the best view of the Teton Range, you can stay at Colter Bay RV Park or Colter Bay Campground. Another choice is to stay at Lizard Creek Campground because it's only 11 miles away from Yellowstone and 8 miles from Colter Bay Village, which gives you convenient access (*Camping*, 2022).

Exciting Activities to Do

Have you decided to take your next vacation to Grand Teton? When planning your trip to this park, you will want to incorporate various activities, whether you're going by yourself or with your family. There are actually a lot of things to do here, but mostly during the summer. If you have no idea what to choose, here are some exciting options.

Hiking

Grand Teton National Park is undoubtedly one of the best destinations for hiking in North America. From its beautiful lakes to its amazing mountain range, hiking is a great way to immerse yourself in nature. From the hiking trails, many animals like bears and bison are regularly spotted by visitors. If you want to discover the best spots to view the scenery at Grand Teton, it's time to pack your bag and have an adventure by exploring the various hiking trails.

However, you might not know where to go first since the park is so large. In this section, I'll give you a list of the hiking trails within Grand Teton. Starting with the easy hiking trails, this list will move on to longer and harder trails. All of them can be finished in a single day, so you won't have to worry about camping or staying the night. Additionally, there are some short trails that you may even combine to explore more places.

Easy Day Hikes

Trail	Description
Taggart Lake	This is an easy trail with a distance of 3.8 miles, which will only take 1 to 3 hours to complete. It's one of the best spots to see the scenery of the Teton Range.

Phelps Lake Overlook	With a distance of only 2 miles, this trail can be finished in an hour or less. This easy trail is great if you want to take a walk with your family.
Heron Pond at Swan Lake Loop Trail	The distance is 3.2 miles, which only takes 2 to 3 hours to complete. With this trail, you'll find yourself walking through the wetlands and trees to view the mountain range.
Lunch Tree Hill	This is the shortest and easiest one on this list because it's only 0.5 miles and can be completed in about 45 minutes or even less. This one is perfect if you have kids with you.
Lake Creek at Woodland Trail Loop	The distance is 3.3 miles, which can be completed in 1 to 3 hours. This is an easy trail that passes through the Phelp Lake's shore.

Moderate Day Hikes

Trail	Description
Taggart and Bradley Lakes	This moderate hike will take 3 to 4 hours to complete. Through this trail, you can view the two lakes at the same time. Hikers usually pass this trail right after the Taggart

	Lake Trail.
Jenny Lake Loop	This loop trail is 7.9 miles in distance and takes 3 to 5 hours to finish. Like the name, not only will you view the scenery of Jenny Lake but also Cascade Canyon.
Aspen Ridge—Boulder Ridge	This is a moderate trail that is 6.1 miles long. You'll need 3 to 5 hours to finish this loop. You'll pass through the Aspen and Boulder Ridges before arriving at Phelps Lake.
Hermitage Point	This is a long trail with a 9.7-mile distance. It will take you around 4 to 7 hours from start to finish. You'll walk through the meadows and forests and see the Teton Range's scenery.
Forks of Cascade Canyon	The distance is 9.1 miles with a duration of 5 to 9 hours. As the name suggests, this hike passes through the Cascade Canyon. Along this trail, you may spot animals like bears and moose.

Trail	Description
Marion Lake	This is a difficult trail with a distance of 5.1 miles, which takes you around 9 to 13 hours to complete. Before reaching Marion Lake, the trail passes a number of ridges both up and down. But on the way, you'll see incredible views of the meadows full of flowers.
Death Canyon—Static Peak Divide Junction	This is a challenging but rewarding hike that's 16.8 miles long, which may take you around 9 to 11 hours. This extremely difficult trail offers breathtaking landscapes along with chances to see wild animals. However, it's not recommended if you have heart or respiratory conditions.
Lake Solitude	This is a strenuous trail with a distance of 16.6 miles, which will take you 8 to 12 hours to finish. This challenging hike can be rewarding for experienced hikers. You'll pass through Lake Solitude and also view the Cascade Canyon.
Paintbrush Canyon—Cascade Canyon Loop	This is the longest trail at Grand Teton, with a 20-mile loop distance. But it gives the most

	amazing scenery of the park through Paintbrush and Cascade Canyons as well as Lake Solitude. However, you must know that it will take 11 to 14 hours to finish it.
Surprise and Amphitheater Lakes	The distance of this trail is 10.1 miles, which can be completed in 6 to 7 hours. While walking through this, you'll experience the beautiful mountain views. However, you'll pass through the thick forest where there is often bear activity.

Hiking Tips at Grand Teton

After finding out all the trails available at Grand Teton, have you decided on what to choose first? If so, it's time to put on your hiking shoes and pack your bag for the hike. To make your hike easier, here's a list of tips to follow when hiking at the park:

- During the summer, these hiking trails will be packed with visitors. To avoid crowds, you should wake up before the sun rises and start your hike earlier than other hikers.

- Since you might hike to remote areas that have no cell service, you should bring a map of the trails or download it on your smartphone.

- The weather at Grand Teton might change from time to time. Prior to your hike, you should check the latest conditions for accurate information.

- Since there are many bears in Grand Teton, you must take precautions by bringing bear spray and staying away when you spot them on the trail.

- You should prepare your body for a challenging hike because many trails have high elevations and steep paths.

- You must always bring safety gear when hiking in case unwanted situations happen.

- Because wildlife is often active along the trails, you must not bring your pet to avoid getting attacked.

Boating and Floating

Finding ways to stay cool is essential for savoring your summer as temperatures increase. If you enjoy water activities, there are many beautiful lakes and rivers at Grand Teton you can go to. However, if you want to go boating, you must know that you need to have a permit and the appropriate skills. Water activities can be dangerous, no matter your level of experience. This means that you must be aware of safety rules for boating or other activities within Grand Teton.

When you bring your own boat to the park, you need to apply for a permit at Recreation.gov. Moreover, there is a fee that you have to pay for a permit, which is $75 for a motorized boat and $25 for a nonmotorized one, like a kayak, raft, or canoe (*Get on the water*, 2023). However, if you don't want to bring your own boat, you can still rent a kayak or canoe at the park for at least two hours. Not only that, but there are also rafts for rent if you'd rather float than play in the water by yourself.

Furthermore, there are some regulations you need to follow while doing these water activities, as follows:

- It's prohibited to get in the water after drinking alcohol or taking drugs.

- You must pack up your trash after your activity.

- You may only water ski around Jackson Lake.

- It's not permitted to light a fire around the Snake River.

- You can't bring pets to other lakes or rivers except for Jackson Lake.

Biking at Grand Teton

If you don't want to drive or even hike at Grand Teton, biking can be a great option for you. This activity may also help you spend time with your family without having to depend on cars or other vehicles. Not only will you get to exercise, but you'll also see various stunning views of the park, such as the mountain range and green fields. However, you need to be aware that there might be wildlife activity along the path, so you must be careful and reduce your speed when you come across it. If you can't bring your own bike, there are some vendors that offer bikes for rent. Another important thing to note is that you need to pay a fee for biking in the park.

Moreover, the options for biking at Grand Teton are virtually limitless since there are paved roads that can't be entered by other vehicles. For instance, there is a bike trail in Jackson Hole that stretches for over 70 miles (Liz, 2020). On this pathway, you'll see the scenery of beautiful landscapes like horse ranches and mountain views from various angles. Even though biking is not a dangerous activity, you still need to take precautions to keep yourself safe. I've explained some biking safety measures in Chapter 1, but I'll add some more in this section.

- When you're about to cross a street, you must let the drivers know by using hand signals.

- You shouldn't ride your bike too fast; instead maintain your speed at an acceptable level.

- When you get off the bike, you must not leave food or other belongings behind in case animals attempt to approach it.

Fishing

Another popular activity you should try at Grand Teton is fishing. If you enjoy fishing accompanied by beautiful views of the mountains and lakes, the park is the perfect place. There are many rivers, streams, and lakes to choose from if you decide to do this. However, before you can fish, Wyoming state law governs fishing regulations within the park, so you need to get a fishing license.

Prior to your fishing trip, you should also check the season dates of the rivers, streams, and lakes. The lakes are open for fishing all year long, except for Jackson, which closes in October. In the rivers and streams, you must return every cutthroat trout taken in the Snake River from early November to the end of March (*Fishing*, 2022). Before going, you must find out updated information about closures in case there is one.

When planning a fishing trip at Grand Teton, you must want to fish at the best places. Here, I'll let you know the top destinations:

- **Snake River:** This is the most popular spot for fishing at the park because numerous native fish species inhabit it. The most known fish species is the cutthroat trout, which originates in this river (Durrant, 2023).

- **Jenny Lake:** This lake is not only good for water activities like boating and kayaking but also a great spot for fishing. Some fish species you may find here are lake and brook trout.

- **Pacific Creek:** If you don't want to fish in a big body of water, this small stream can be your option. Since the creek is connected directly to the Snake River, you'll also find cutthroat trout.

- **Jackson Lake:** If you wish to catch big fish, Jackson is the perfect place for that. It's said that someone was able to catch a

50-pound lake trout in this lake (Durrant, 2023). However, this lake is always packed with visitors, so it's not great for those who like solitude when fishing.

- **Gros Ventre River:** This is another busy and popular spot at Grand Teton. Cutthroat trout from the Snake River can also be found here. It's great for fishing in July because salmon flies begin to hatch.

Climbing

If you enjoy a more extreme activity, climbing is a great option. Each year, many visitors attempt to reach the various mountain peaks at Grand Teton. However, this sport is not for the faint of heart because it can be dangerous if you're not experienced or careful with your planning and preparation. You don't need to have a climbing permit for this activity, but if you plan to stay overnight, you must apply for a backcountry camping permit at Jenny Lake Ranger Station (*Climbing and mountaineering*, 2019).

Before planning a climbing trip, you have to take safety precautions because some risks can present themselves, such as extreme weather, avalanches, rockfalls, and floods. Let's go over some safety tips:

- The most important thing is to make sure that your body is in a healthy condition before the climb to avoid getting sick.

- You must always check the surrounding conditions before climbing by asking the staff at a visitor center.

- Since the weather on the mountain may change at any time, you should prepare additional clothing to warm your body.

- You have to understand your own limits. It's very difficult to reach the mountain peaks, so you shouldn't try to climb the hardest one if you have no experience.

- To solve unexpected events, you need to create an elaborate plan. For example, you should prepare what to do if someone gets hurt or when the weather suddenly shifts.

- You need to prepare the proper climbing equipment. If you fail to bring the right gear for climbing, you might get into an accident and injure yourself. You must also learn how to use them the right way.

Wildlife Watching

Since the animal populations at Grand Teton are very diverse, it's also great for watching wildlife. Some animals you can often see in the parks are moose, bears, pronghorn, bison, and more. A few of the best spots for wildlife viewing in the park are Oxbow Bend, Mormon Row, Cascade Canyon, Snake River, and Timbered Island (John, 2021).

However, before doing this activity, you should know that you need to maintain a safe distance from the animals. These are wild animals which makes it hard to predict their movements and actions. If you approach them, they might attack and injure you. Here are some safety tips to follow while watching wildlife at Grand Teton:

- You should never stand between the animals and their offspring because they might get defensive and attack you.

- You need to avoid harassing or disturbing the animals since human contact may negatively affect them over time, causing them to become stressed.

- You must watch your behaviors and actions during the wildlife viewing so that other visitors can enjoy the trip.

Key Takeaways

- Grand Teton National Park got its name from the word "Teton," which means breast in French.

- The park is located in Wyoming and was first established in 1929.

- The park has a rich human history that dates back to over 11,000 years ago.

- The most famous destinations at Grand Teton are Jenny Lake, Inspiration Point, Hidden Falls, and Mormon Row.

- When planning your trip, you need to know basic information like its opening seasons and hours, fees and passes, permits, accommodations, and campgrounds.

- During the summer, there are a lot of exciting activities to do, such as hiking, boating, floating, biking, fishing, climbing, and wildlife viewing.

In the next chapter, you'll find out about everything to know about Yosemite National Park.

Chapter 3:

Yosemite National Park

Did you know that Yosemite may be the third national park in the United States, but it was the one that sparked the concept? Over two decades before it was established as a national park, President Lincoln approved the Yosemite Land Grant in 1864 to secure and protect Yosemite Valley and Mariposa Grove (Peglar, 2021a). We still reap the rewards of the government's action to this day since it was the first time they safeguarded and protected land due to its natural beauty. If you're ready to start exploring national parks, Yosemite is one of the most beautiful ones there is.

History and Culture

Yosemite National Park was officially established in 1890 and is situated in the Sierra Nevada region of California (Peglar, 2021a). Yosemite's landscape was formed because of the clashes between glaciers and rocks (*The history of Yosemite National Park*, 2023). Granite makes up the majority of the park's distinctive formations of rock. This is why you can discover different stunning rock formations all over the park. However, Yosemite is not just about rock. There are a lot of other things to see, such as beautiful lakes, canyons, and waterfalls.

Seven thousand to ten thousand years before the Europeans came across the land, Yosemite was home to Native Americans who called themselves the Ahwahnechee (*Yosemite Park history, timeline, and evolution*). Actually, the name "Yosemite" came from the word "Ahwahnee," which was mispronounced by the Europeans. These people survived on the land by gathering plants and hunting animals. However, they were relocated to a reservation after the settlers discovered gold in California.

You might be wondering what Yosemite is known for and what the most famous attractions in the park are. The first one is Yosemite Falls. This is said to be the highest waterfall in the country, standing at 2,424 feet high (Singh, 2023). Since it's surrounded by a mountain range, many visitors hike one of the peaks to get the best view of Yosemite Falls. However, the water might change depending on the season, and during times of drought, there will be no water at all. Before visiting, you must check what the conditions are first. The best time to visit is in spring.

Another famous attraction at Yosemite is Half Dome. I've mentioned before that there are many rock formations in the park, and this is one of them. This granite formation is 4,737 feet tall and is a great place for those who enjoy rock climbing (Singh, 2023). However, the way to the peak is very strenuous and challenging to reach. If you don't want to climb it, there are many viewpoints in the valley to view Half Dome.

Glacier Point is also a popular destination in the park. It's a lookout point overlooking Yosemite Valley. From this attraction, you'll be able to see various sights within the park, like Yosemite Falls and Half Dome. To reach it, you can walk or drive. But because the path has a high elevation, most visitors prefer to take a bus to make it easier.

Yosemite also has very diverse wildlife, with over 400 species of animals (*Animals*, 2017). There are predators that roam the forested areas and small creatures that fly over the sky, which makes the park the perfect place for wildlife viewing. Some wild animals that inhabit the park are black bears, mountain lions, mule deer, coyotes, bighorn sheep, red foxes, and more. These animals create their own habitats, from the thick forests to the green meadows.

Basic Information

If you've chosen Yosemite as your next destination, there are a couple of things you need to know: First, from its operating hours and seasons to its various campgrounds available. In this part, I'll inform you about each of them.

Operating Seasons and Hours

Yosemite opens its gate all year long, 24 hours a day. You might also ask which season is the best to visit the park, but it all depends on what activities you want to do. For example, if you want to hike or climb, it's better to do it in the summer or spring. However, if you wish to go skiing or snowboarding, you'll have to visit during the winter months. As a note, there will be some roads and attractions that are closed in the winter, so you must check for updates before your trip.

There are five different visitor centers in the park situated in Yosemite Valley, as follows:

1. **Valley Visitor Center:** This one opens its door all year long and provides various facilities, such as an information center, a bookstore, and an exhibition of the park's history.

2. **Tuolumne Meadows Visitor Center:** This one is only open to visitors during the summer season. This visitor center offers an exhibition about Yosemite's wildlife, geology, human history, and more.

3. **Wawona Information Center:** The operating hours of this visitor center vary, so you must check online first. You can find information about the park's activities here, as well as apply for wilderness permits.

4. **Valley Wilderness Center:** This one is only open to visitors from May to October. You can find maps as well as guidebooks and get wilderness permits from here.

5. **Big Oak Flat Information Station:** The information desk has a staff that can answer your questions about the park. In this visitor center, you can get maps, guidebooks, and permits.

Fees and Passes

Before entering Yosemite, you're required to purchase a park pass first at the entrance. Except for the Hetch Hetchy entrance, other park entrances are open 24/7 to visitors, so you won't have to worry about what time you arrive. However, you can't pay in cash because the park only accepts mobile payment methods as well as credit and debit cards. The standard entrance pass is priced at $20 to $35 per person or vehicle. If you wish to enter the park multiple times a year, you can purchase an annual pass for only $70.

Permits

There are some activities or events where a permit is necessary. Here are some permits required for special activities:

- **Half Dome permit:** If you want to hike or climb the top of this rock formation, you will need a permit. Each day, only 300 visitors get to hike on this trail (*Half Dome permits*, 2023).

- **Wilderness permit:** If you plan to stay overnight in the park wilderness, you must get a permit first. Since climbing and hiking are very popular at Yosemite, and most stay overnight, the park management has a daily quota for each trail to avoid overcrowding.

- **Special Use permits:** Some events you need a permit for are weddings, filming events, scattering of ashes, and church ceremonies.

- **Business and Commercial Use permits:** If you wish to work with the park management and open a company at Yosemite, you'll need to get a permit. For example, if you want to lead guiding activities like hiking or fishing or do photography professionally.

Accommodations

Are you planning to stay overnight at Yosemite? Then, you must find yourself a suitable and comfortable accommodation. There are some lodges available within the park, and every one of them is managed by

Yosemite management. Here is a list of lodging options within Yosemite:

- **Yosemite Valley Lodge:** If the attraction you're most excited to see is Yosemite Falls, then this lodge is a great place for you. It's also a fantastic option for those who visit with their family or in big groups. Its wood and glass design blends well with the landscape. Moreover, the lodge's large windows also let in plenty of Yosemite's breathtaking scenery. It also offers different kinds of facilities like bike rentals, shuttle access, daily housekeeping, and more. However, you're not allowed to bring pets here.

- **The Ahwahnee:** This is a popular accommodation because it has beautiful interior and building designs. The lodge was established with the goal of showcasing the attractions surrounding it, which include Glacier Point and Half Dome. It provides its guests with many things, like a gift shop, heated swimming pool, and valet parking.

- **Curry Village:** This is a lodging option that's close to Glacier Point. It offers various types of accommodations like tents, cabins, and hotel rooms. It also has a gift shop, shuttle access, in-house restaurants, and so on.

- **Wawona Hotel:** Situated close to Mariposa Grove, this is a standard hotel that has over 100 rooms with private or shared bathrooms. You may get your breakfast, lunch, and dinner in their dining area, which means that you won't have to worry about finding another restaurant. Some amenities provided here are a golf course, hiking trails, a swimming pool, and more.

- **White Wolf Lodge:** This lodge is set up remotely for those who enjoy peace and quiet. It's also surrounded by meadows filled with flowers. It offers its guests over 20 tents and wood cabins. However, you're not allowed to cook by yourself to prevent wild animals from approaching the property.

- **Housekeeping Camp:** Do you want to sleep outdoors but are too lazy to bring your own tent? Then, this one's for you. It offers something like concrete buildings but with canvas covering the top and sides. Around the property, you'll experience the beautiful scenery of Half Dome and Yosemite Falls.

- **High Sierra Camps:** This one is made for backpackers because it's located in the wilderness. You'll reach this accommodation by walking or riding a mule so that you can explore the backcountry areas of Yosemite. The camps are spread in various areas, including Vogelsang, Merced Lake, May Lake, Sunrise, Glen Aulin, and Tuolumne Meadows (Lodging, 2022).

- **Glacier Point Ski Hut:** This accommodation is open during the winter months, December through March. Yosemite Falls and Half Dome vistas are also visible from here. It's a rustic-style lodge that offers comfortable couches and rooms with bunk beds.

- **Tuolumne Meadows Lodge:** This lodge provides its guests with tent cabins. It's only open during the summer months, which are June through September. Those who are planning to hike or backpack through the park often stop here as well.

However, if you can't reserve a room in time, you may also find one in the neighboring areas.

Campgrounds

If you enjoy camping more than staying in a hotel room, Yosemite offers some campgrounds all over the park. From April to October, you need to make a reservation to get a campsite at these campgrounds. However, getting a reservation can be difficult because the campgrounds are always packed with visitors. This means that if you are planning on visiting during the summer, you should book a campsite as soon as you can. If you wish to camp in fall, winter, or spring, there are campgrounds you can reserve on the spot with a first-come, first-serve method.

Here, I'll list the campgrounds available at Yosemite, along with its price. However, please note that these are the current prices, so you'll want to check online for more accurate information.

Yosemite Valley

Name	Price (Nightly)
Camp 4	$10 per person
North Pines	$36
Lower Pines	$36
Upper Pines	$36

North of Yosemite Valley

Name	Price (Nightly)
Tuolumne Meadows	$36
Porcupine Flat	$20
Hodgdon Meadow	$36
Yosemite Creek	$24

Crane Flat	$36
White Wolf	$30
Tamarack Flat	$24

South of Yosemite Valley

Name	Price (Nightly)
Bridalveil Creek	$36
Wawona	$36

Campground Information

Currently, Yosemite Creek and White Wolf Campgrounds are not open for visitors. Tuolumne Meadows Campground is also closed until 2024 0r 2025 because of rehabilitation activities managed by the park (*Campgrounds*, 2023). This means you must choose another one if you've thought about going to one of these campgrounds. There are also some facilities available in these campgrounds, as follows:

- There are dump stations near Wawona, Tuolumne Meadows, and Upper Pines Campgrounds.

- There are showers at Curry Village that you need to pay for. This is the only place showers can be accessed.

- Creek or tap water can be found at these campgrounds. If a campground has creek water, it will also have vault toilets.

Summer Activities

Are you ready for your summer vacation? The greatest time of year to visit Yosemite is during the summer months. If you plan to visit the park in the summer months, you need to organize some fun activities, whether you're traveling solo or with your friends and family. In this section, I'll provide you with a few summer activities to immerse yourself in the nature of Yosemite National Park.

Hiking a Trail

If you want to relax and enjoy the beautiful views of Yosemite, hiking a trail can be your option. Whether you're a beginner or an experienced hiker, the park offers various trails according to your level. Here, I'll give you 11 known hiking trails inside of Yosemite, along with their difficulty levels and lengths.

Easy Day Hikes

Trail	Description
Cook's Meadow Loop	This trail takes you through a meadow. It's located in the heart of Yosemite Valley, which makes it easier to see the views of Yosemite Falls and Half Dome. This is an easy hike since it's 1 mile long and only takes about 30 minutes to finish. However, the trail is not recommended in the winter because it can be slippery and wet.

Lower Yosemite Falls	If you wish to see the beautiful view of Yosemite Falls, this trail is a wonderful choice. This is considered an easy trail because it's only 1 mile long, which only takes you 30 minutes to an hour to complete. The best time to do this hike is from May to July.
Bridalveil Fall	This is an easy and short hike that takes you to Bridalveil Falls. With a distance of 0.5 miles, you can finish this trail in around 15 to 20 minutes. The trail is also paved, which is very convenient for those who don't enjoy a difficult hike.

Moderate Day Hikes

Trail	Description
Valley Loop	This trail is located in the western part of Yosemite Valley. You'll walk through the meadows and forests on this trail, which is great if you enjoy solitude. This loop is 11.5 miles long with a duration of 5 to 7 hours. Along the path, you'll also see the views of Cathedral Rocks, Yosemite Falls, and El Capitan.
Mirror Lake Loop	You'll walk along the shore of Mirror Lake and overlook the view of Half Dome. Not only

	that, but you may also see the scenery of Washington Column and Tenaya Canyon. This trail is a 5-mile loop that will take you 2 to 3 hours to finish.
Vernal and Nevada Falls	This is a moderate trail that offers close-up views of Vernal and Nevada Falls. You'll also see a variety of geological features along the way, which makes the hike more exciting. This hike is 7 miles long, which will take you 2 to 5 hours to complete.
Panorama Trail	This is a great trail to see Glacier and Panorama Points. This hike is very long, with over 8 miles of path one way. It will take you 4 to 7 hours to complete this.

Strenuous Day Hikes

Trail	Description
Four Mile	This is a strenuous but rewarding trail since you'll find yourself reaching the famous Glacier Point. With a distance of 9.4 miles, you'll need 2 to 5 hours for a one-way trip. If you want to challenge yourself, this trail is a great option.

Half Dome	It's a strenuous hike that is around 15 miles long. This trail is not recommended if you are out of shape or have heart or respiratory issues. Most people can finish this hike in around 10 to 12 hours.
Snow Creek	This one is situated beyond the Mirror Lake trail. Along the path, you'll also see the view of Tenaya Canyon. This hike is 9.4 miles long with a duration of 6 to 7 hours.
Upper Yosemite Falls	You can view Yosemite Falls from the base or the top. This trail allows you to hike to Yosemite Falls' peak to get the best scenery. However, this hike is very challenging because it's 7.6 miles long, which takes you 6 to 10 hours to finish.

Taking a Guided Bus Tour

If you want to save your energy while exploring Yosemite, taking a guided bus tour is the perfect choice. There are many experienced tour guides who will teach you all the knowledge about the park's history, popular attractions, wildlife, and more. Every tour will take around 2 hours and can be taken in either an open-air tram to enjoy the wind of the summer months or a heated motor bus with glass windows in the cold winter (*Guided bus tours*, 2023). This is also a great idea for those traveling with older people or young kids to enjoy the scenery of Yosemite without too much strenuous activity. Some tours to choose from are Glacier Point, Yosemite Grand, and Yosemite Valley Floor Tours. The following are more details about the tour:

- You may reserve a ticket online and pick it up at the Yosemite Valley Lodge Front Desk 15 minutes before the time.

- Since many tours are available during the summer, your tram or bus tour might take longer to finish because of traffic.

- You should arrive at the Yosemite Valley Lodge 15 minutes before the departure because the tour will not wait for late passengers.

- If you come to the park in your own vehicle, you need to arrive much earlier to get a parking spot.

Biking at Yosemite

Another way to enjoy the natural landscapes of Yosemite is by biking. By doing this, you may avoid the hassles of traffic in the summer. By allowing you to take in the views rather than merely driving past them, it might provide you with an entirely different viewpoint on the surrounding landscapes. You don't even need to look for a big parking spot whenever you wish to stop at a destination.

There is a set path made for biking with over 12 miles of paved roads (*Explore on two wheels*, 2023). However, you're not allowed to bike on hiking trails or sidewalks. Along the way on the bike trail, you'll discover various things like gift shops, nature centers, museums, and more. Another important thing to keep in mind is that according to California law, you need to wear a helmet if you're over 18 years old (*Ride a bike*, 2021).

What if you didn't bring your own bike? You can rent one in the park! There are three rental locations, including Yosemite and Curry Villages, as well as Yosemite Valley Lodge. The price for the bike also differs, starting at only $30.

Watching Birds

If you enjoy watching birds, you can do so at Yosemite. The park is inhabited by over 265 species of birds (*Birdwatching*, 2023). Birds are drawn to it because of its diverse environment, which includes streams, woods, rivers, and meadows. Some bird species you'll discover here are the American robin, mountain chickadee, and Steller's jay (Provozin, 2022a). However, you'll see more bright-colored birds during the fall and spring seasons flying over the wet meadows. Additionally, some of the most popular birds that birdwatchers go after here are pileated woodpecker, spotted owl, and northern goshawk.

If you're still a beginner and unsure how to start birdwatching, the park offers tours led by an expert who will share their knowledge and take you to the best destinations to see birds. But if you'd like to do it by yourself, you can walk to various hotspots around to hear their lovely and melodious sounds. A few popular spots for birdwatching are Stockton Creek Preserve, White Rock Road, and Bean Creek Preserve.

However, the most important thing to note is to follow birding etiquette. The forests and meadows are typically tranquil and quiet, so you must refrain from walking or talking loudly while birdwatching. You also need to avoid disturbing or feeding the birds human food.

Fishing

I've mentioned that there are various rivers, streams, and lakes located within Yosemite National Park. This means that you'll get to experience fishing on another level. Whether you wish to relax or make memories with your loved ones, fishing is a fun activity while visiting the park. However, you'll have to get a California fishing license if you're over 16 years old, which you can apply for online (Provozin, 2022b). The fishing season at Yosemite lasts for over six months, from the end of April to the middle of November. Furthermore, you need to ensure that you've followed the park's fishing regulations beforehand.

The most common fish you'll find here are rainbow trout, crappie, brookie, and brown trout. If you're not sure where to fish, a few popular spots for fishing are Tenaya Lake, Merced River, Hetch Hetchy Reservoir, Eleanor Lake, and Tuolumne River (Provozin, 2022b).

Riding a Horse or Mule

If you want to do an anti-mainstream activity at Yosemite, you can opt for horseback or mule riding. This is also one of the best ways to explore the park since you'll be provided with a tour guide who can share their knowledge and take you to the hotspots of Yosemite. The park offers a two-hour ride with a mule or horse that you can take from Wawona Stable. No prior experience is required for this tour, but your body must be healthy to avoid unwanted accidents since there are difficult pathways along the way. From the stable, this tour will take you through the Meadow Loop Trail and back.

Let's take a look at some important details for horseback and mule riding:

- The fee for this tour is $85 per person for a two-hour ride.

- You must be 7 years old or over.

- You must wear footwear that covers your toes.

- It's essential to wear long pants during the tour.

- You can't bring your bags, so you need to leave them in your car.

- If your trip to Yosemite is in the summer, it's best to reserve a morning tour to avoid excessive heat in the afternoon.

Rock Climbing

In the History and Culture section, I mentioned that Yosemite is made up of many rock formations. The most famous one is Half Dome, which is a granite rock structure. This means that the park has become one of the greatest destinations for rock climbing. Climbers will face various kinds of challenges here because there are many rock formations to climb. This activity is also considered somewhat extreme since you'll need prior experience before taking it on, and your body has to be very fit to overcome the terrain.

However, because there have been a lot of climbers over the years, the effects of climbing are getting considerably more apparent. A few of these effects involve erosion, trash, water pollution, and more. This is why the park management enforces strict rules for climbers in the hope that future generations can still experience the beauty of these rock formations. The following are some regulations you must adhere to:

- After climbing, you must pick up your trash to keep the site clean.

- If you plan to stay the night while climbing, you have to apply for a wilderness permit.

- You must bring proper gear to avoid getting into accidents because a rescue operation is dangerous and expensive.

- You shouldn't enter closed areas, so you need to keep yourself updated.

- You need to store your food well to prevent wild animals from approaching it.

- If you see another person breaking these rules, you can remind them of the consequences of their actions.

Stargazing

We know how difficult it is to see stars in the city because of all the lights. If you enjoy looking at the stars, Yosemite is the perfect place. Every year, many people choose this nighttime activity and gaze at the sky to watch billions of stars. The park also provides a variety of tours for stargazing. There'll be tour guides who will teach you about various things like constellations, meteors, and planets. Additionally, they'll take you to the best spots for this activity. You should also bring your binoculars and charts about stars and constellations. Some of the best places for stargazing at Yosemite are as follows:

- **Glacier Point:** During the day, this place is great to look at Yosemite Valley and Half Dome. However, it's also one of the best places to stargaze in the evening because of its clear view of the east.

- **Fresno Dome:** This is also a popular rock formation at Yosemite. Since it has great views over the sky, it's a known spot to stargaze and look at the full moon.

- **Tunnel View:** This is a good option since you'll be able to see the views of Half Dome and Bridalveil Fall. During the night, the sky over it is so clear to watch the stars.

Rafting

Another fun water activity to do at Yosemite is rafting. The most popular destination for this is the Merced River. Rafting gives you the time to relax and cool off while enjoying the stunning views of the park. The best seasons for rafting are in spring after the snow has melted and in summer when you want to avoid the hot days. Rafting is also influenced by variables like the water temperature and depth of the river. The park offers visitors raft rentals to go down the Merced River for only $30.50 per person (*Meander down the Merced River*, 2023). Typically, each raft can be filled with two to four people.

However, you must be careful and take safety precautions when doing a water activity to avoid unexpected situations. The following are some safety tips:

- This activity requires good swimming ability.

- Rafting is not recommended for kids under 50 lbs.

- You can't bring alcohol while rafting.

- You're not allowed to tie rafts to one another.

- Your life jacket must be worn throughout the activity.

- You should put your belongings in a waterproof bag.

Winter Activities

If you plan to come to Yosemite during the winter, there are also some fun activities to choose from. In this section, let's explore each of them before deciding which one you'd like to do.

Cross-Country Snowshoeing and Skiing

If you enjoy these winter activities, Yosemite offers some of the most breathtaking trails that pass through the mountains and other popular destinations in the park. Since there's a blanket of snow covering the plants, these winter activities offer an environmentally beneficial and enjoyable way to explore the park. This means that you won't have to worry about affecting or hurting the plants when walking. Since these activities can be done only in the winter, you may visit Yosemite from December to March.

However, it can be difficult to find the trails since snow frequently covers paths and markings. The park management typically uses a metal sign connected to a tree to give directions, so you must pay attention to avoid getting lost (*Winter activities*, 2023). The trail starts at the Badger Pass Ski Area, where you can discover over 90 miles of paths equipped with signs (*Cross-country skiing*, 2023).

Ice Skating

Yosemite has been a famous winter destination since 1929 because of ice skating (*Winter activities*, 2023). The park even provides visitors with an ice rink in the Curry Village area. From this ice rink, you'll also see the view of Half Dome, which makes ice skating much more exciting. There is a fee you need to pay for skating in the ice rink, which is $15 for kids and $16 for adults. You will have two hours to play around and have fun. Also, don't forget to put on your helmet, which will be provided by the rental place.

Downhill Snowboarding and Skiing

This is also another option if you enjoy skiing and snowboarding. The trail for these activities is also located in the Badger Pass Ski Area. The rental place to rent equipment for skiing and snowboarding is open from December to March. However, the operating hours also depend on the snow and weather conditions. The rental place also provides experienced instructors for those who want to learn. To do these activities, you'll need to pay. Rates start at $5, depending on your age and the length of your stay. Moreover, equipment like helmets, skis, snowboards, and boots can also be rented starting at $9.50.

Snow Tubing and Sledding

If you're visiting with your family, snow tubing can be a great option for everyone. The Badger Pass Ski Area offers a snow tubing path that is kid-friendly, so you can go down the slope safely, even with your children. However, children need to be over 42 inches tall for this activity (*Snow tubing*, 2023). Additionally, the fee to rent a snow tube starts at $30 for each person.

Furthermore, sledding is not allowed at the Badger Pass Ski Area. But there are some other snow play areas for this activity located in the Leland High Sierra and Tenaya at the south entrance.

Key Takeaways

- Yosemite National Park was founded in 1890.

- It's located in the Sierra Nevada region of California.

- Yosemite was named after the word "Ahwahnee."

- The most popular attractions in the park are Yosemite Falls, Half Dome, and Glacier Point.

- Some essential details to know before visiting Yosemite are its operating seasons and hours, fees and passes, permits, accommodations, and campgrounds.

- In the summer, there are a lot of activities to do, such as hiking a trail, taking guided bus tours, biking, birdwatching, fishing, mule or horseback riding, rock climbing, stargazing, and rafting.

- Yosemite also offers winter activities, such as cross-country snowshoeing and skiing, ice skating, downhill snowboarding and skiing, and snow tubing, as well as sledding.

In Chapter 4, we'll discuss the Grand Canyon National Park. Before your visit, I'll let you know everything you need to prepare.

Chapter 4:

Grand Canyon National Park

Did you know that the Grand Canyon, located inside Grand Canyon National Park, is nominated as one of the World's Seven Natural Wonders (Dierickx, 2015)? To this day, it continues to rank as the busiest and most visited national park in the United States.

History and Culture

Grand Canyon National Park lies in the northern region of Arizona and was officially founded as a national park in 1919 (Onion et al., 2020). It's believed that the canyon was created over 5 million years ago as the Colorado River carved a passage over rock formations, which ended up creating the Grand Canyon's structures (*Grand Canyon history*, 2023). The Spanish were the first to find the canyon while looking for a gold mine. However, the next explorers who were able to reach the Grand Canyon arrived over two centuries later.

The park had been occupied by Native American tribes for more than 10,000 years prior to the arrival of the Spanish explorers (*Grand Canyon history*, 2023). This made the region full of human history and culture. These inhabitants used the park to establish their homes, hunt wild animals, and forage their food. Some tribes who were living in the Grand Canyon were the Pueblo and Havasupai people, as well as the tribes of Navajo, Hopi, Paiute, and Zuni (Onion et al., 2020). To this day, these people still consider the area as their ancestral home and try to preserve the history as best as they can.

What are among the most well-known sights in Grand Canyon National Park? The first one is Mather Point. This is one of the most famous lookout points among visitors. It's also very easy to reach since you only have to take a short walk from the main visitor center. The best hours to visit it are early in the morning to see the sunrise and late in the afternoon to watch the sunset. Since it's not difficult to reach, Mather Point is packed with people all day long.

Another known destination is the South Rim area. This region is popular because it offers many activities for outdoor enthusiasts, such as mule rides, guided tours, and hiking trails. There are also some lookout points to see over the whole canyon. Biking or running in this area is also great because you'll see stunning views. However, the South Rim region is often filled with visitors, so it's recommended to arrive here early in the morning.

Additionally, Desert View Drive is also a popular attraction. You can take a drive here with your car to see the views of the Colorado River and the Grand Canyon (Parker, 2023a). It attracts many visitors because it offers various stunning lookout points and picnic areas. The Desert View Watchtower is also situated within this area so that you can stop by during your drive.

Grand Canyon National Park is home to diverse animal populations. There are hundreds of animal species inhabiting the area, from mammals to birds. It's said that there are 450 species of birds, 18 species of fish, 91 species of mammals, 58 species of reptiles, and 1,443 species of invertebrates (*Park statistics*, 2023). Some animals you can discover here are mule deer, golden eagles, bighorn sheep, blue jays, bobcats, and more. Not only that, but the park also has a diverse vegetation population with over 2,000 species living in its soil.

Basic Information

Are you ready to go to Grand Canyon National Park on your next vacation? When arranging your itinerary, there is some basic information you have to know first, from its operating hours and seasons to its various lodging options. In this section, let's discuss them to make sure your vacation goes smoothly.

Operating Seasons and Hours

The South Rim area is accessible to visitors 24/7, every day of the year, and even on holidays. All park facilities are open during summer, fall, and spring. This means that the park is packed with people during these seasons, so you must make reservations before visiting. In the winter, a few roads and facilities are unavailable, so you need to check for updated information. To get around the area, you can take a guided bus or hike tour. If you don't wish to use a tour, you can also explore with the park's free shuttle buses.

Furthermore, the North Rim area is open only in the summer months, from early June to the middle of October, because the weather conditions in the winter can be harsh. All roads are also closed in the winter, and there are no facilities or services provided by the park. When the area is open, most visitors will take a guided hike to explore since many remote areas are challenging to navigate. But you may also get around by yourself by bringing a map of the area to avoid getting lost.

Entrance Fees and Passes

When entering Grand Canyon National Park, you need to pay a fee at the entrance. The park pass will be valid for seven days. With this pass, you may enter the South Rim area all year long and the North Rim region when it's open for the season. The standard entrance fee is $20 to $35, and an annual one is priced at $70. These fees can be paid with debit and credit cards. Moreover, there are three different park entrances to get your pass, including the North Rim Entrance Station, East Entrance Station at the Desert View area, and South Entrance Station close to Tusayan (*Grand Canyon permits and reservations*, 2023).

Permits

Permits are necessary when you want to do special activities or events. The following are a few activities that require a permit:

- **Special Use permits:** Many people come to the Grand Canyon for special events since there are a lot of beautiful spots. Some events that need a permit are weddings, birthdays, and reunions. However, the scattering of ashes is not allowed anymore at the park.

- **Colorado River Trip permits:** If you wish to explore the Colorado River, it's also necessary to get a permit.

- **Photography and Filming permits:** You also need permits for these activities to avoid disrupting other visitors.

- **Backcountry permits:** This one is necessary if you plan to camp overnight anywhere other than North Rim or South Rim campgrounds.

- **Scientific Research permits:** If you want to do research within the Grand Canyon, you need to send your proposal to the park for review.

Accommodations

If you want to stay the night inside or around the park, you need to reserve a room that is most suitable for your needs. In this part, let's explore some of the best accommodations within Grand Canyon National Park and around the area.

Places to Stay in the South Rim

Since this area is always busy all year long, many visitors choose to stay overnight in order to have several days to explore the various attractions. There are some lodging options to choose from, as follows:

- **El Tovar Hotel:** This rustic-style hotel is the oldest hotel at the Grand Canyon, which was founded in 1905 (Peglar, 2018). The accommodation offers 70 cabins equipped with air conditioners and private bathrooms. From this hotel, you may also see beautiful views of the canyon.

- **Kachina Lodge:** Opening in 1971, this lodge is located right beside the canyon, which means that many famous attractions are within walking distance (*Kachina Lodge*, 2015). This accommodation is more like a motel equipped with a fridge, TV, full bath, and more.

- **Yavapai Lodge:** Established in 1958, this hotel is close to the main visitor center and can be reached in less than 10 minutes (Ruland, 2022). Its exterior has a rustic style, while the inside has a modern touch. Some amenities provided are air conditioners, restaurants, and refrigerators.

- **Bright Angel Lodge:** This rustic-style lodge was established in 1935 and nominated as a National Historic Monument (*Bright Angel Lodge and Cabins*, 2020). This accommodation also offers 90 rooms and cabins available for booking.

- **Maswik Lodge:** This lodge was first opened in 1967 and is situated in a ponderosa pine forest (*Maswik Lodge*, 2022). Additionally, there are 90 hotel rooms available. The hotel now also has elevators and some rooms with their own balconies.

- **Thunderbird Lodge:** Established in 1968, this hotel offers comfortable rooms for its guests (*Thunderbird Lodge*, 2015). Some rooms have a direct view over the canyon, which will make your stay more memorable. Some amenities provided here are coffee machines, TVs, and private bathrooms.

A Lodge in the North Rim

If you plan to stay the night in the North Rim area, you can reserve a room at the Grand Canyon Lodge. Since there's only one lodging option here, you must reserve a room a few months to a year before your trip since it's always fully booked.

To get around the North Rim, the lodge provides a mule ride from an hour to half a day. Not only that, but this accommodation also offers some other facilities like a gift shop to purchase souvenirs and a dining room to eat breakfast, dinner, and lunch. Moreover, Roughrider Saloon is a cafe where you can have coffee and baked goods for breakfast and get pizza, as well as cold drinks for lunch and dinner.

An Accommodation at the Bottom of the Canyon

If you're feeling more adventurous and wish to experience a unique accommodation, you may want to stay at the Phantom Ranch. This accommodation is situated at the bottom of the Grand Canyon and the northern part of the Colorado River. It was designed in the 1920s by Mary Jane Colter and constructed with local materials of wood and stone (Peglar, 2023c). This lodge offers its guests dormitories with bunk beds and shared bathrooms.

You can't reach it with a car or any other vehicle since there are no paved roads. There are some ways to find this lodge, which are by walking, riding a mule, or rafting through the river. However, it's not that easy to reach it by foot. Whatever trail you choose, it will take you over four hours to reach. Moreover, what you need to worry about is getting back up since the path is going uphill, which means it has a high elevation.

Places to Stay in the West Rim

If you wish to stay overnight in the West Rim, there are also a couple of lodging options for you. Here are a few accommodations to consider:

- **Hualapai Ranch:** If you like cowboys and Western-style accommodations, this is a great option. They offer cabins that face the canyon, so you will get stunning views during your stay. Not only that, but they also provide some other entertainment like horseback riding, campfires, and wagon rides.

- **Hualapai Lodge:** It serves as the main entry point for tourists who wish to experience the undeveloped canyon landscape. Many would go to this area to hunt, fish, hike, and so on. If you enjoy Native American food, they also have a restaurant that specializes in it called Diamond Creek.

- **Grand Canyon Western Ranch:** This accommodation is created with cowboy decorations and Western-style architecture. It offers cabins and tents decorated with Western furniture. Some facilities here are horseback riding, campfires, and live music.

Accommodations Close to the Grand Canyon

If you don't want to stay in a lodge within the park, there are also some accommodations nearby. Close to the South Rim, there are the towns of Valle, Williams, and Tusayan, where most visitors choose to stay. Here are some recommended hotels in these towns:

- **Grand Canyon Inn:** It takes less than 30 minutes to Grand National Park from this accommodation. The hotel offers some facilities like standard hotel rooms, a bar, a restaurant, and a lounge.

- **Canyon Motel & RV Park:** Located in Williams, this place is only around 50 miles from the Grand Canyon. It offers various types of accommodations, from motel rooms to tents and RV parks, which makes it perfect for everyone. This can be the perfect option for those traveling alone or with their family.

- **Squire Resort at the Grand Canyon:** Situated in Tusayan, this hotel is only about 7 miles away from the canyon. It provides its guests with various facilities, such as swimming pools, restaurants, a bowling alley, and more.

Lodging Close to the Grand Canyon West Rim

If you only want to visit the West Rim area, you may stay the night outside of the park. Many visitors choose to stay in Las Vegas, which is only around 2 hours away, by driving a car or taking a tour. If Las Vegas is too far, there are some closer cities around the West Rim, like Kingman, Laughlin, and Lake Havasu City. These cities are only around 100 miles away from the park.

Campgrounds

If you're an outdoor enthusiast and wish to immerse yourself in nature, you can opt for camping. The park provides some campgrounds in the South Rim and North Rim areas with hundreds of campsites. However, all these campgrounds need to be reserved beforehand to get a spot. Most visitors book one about six months in advance since camping is very popular, especially in the South Rim. Keep in mind that the North Rim is only open in the summer, so you can't camp there during the winter. To reserve a campsite, you can visit Recreation.gov for more information. The following is a list of campgrounds along with their prices:

Campgrounds in the South Rim

Name	Price (Nightly)
Trailer Village RV Park (open all year)	Starting from $64
Mather Campground (open all year)	$18–$50
Desert View (open April through October)	$18

| Ten-X Campground (open May through September) | $20–$175 |

Campgrounds in the North Rim

Name	Price (Nightly)
DeMotte Campground	$26
North Rim Campground	$6–$50

Please be informed that these are the current campsite prices; for more precise information, you need to check online.

Fun Activities to Do

Looking out at the canyon is not the only thing you can do at the Grand Canyon because there are many other activities to put into your itinerary. Whether you're visiting the South Rim or the North Rim when it is in season, you'll never run out of things to do at the park. In this section, I'll list all the fun and exciting things you can do by yourself or with your family.

Hiking

Hiking is a great activity if you wish to unwind and take in the Grand Canyon's breathtaking scenery. There are numerous trails throughout the park that you can choose from, located within the South Rim and North Rim. Here are the most popular hiking routes at the Grand Canyon, along with their lengths and degrees of difficulty.

Trail	Description
South Kaibab to Cedar Ridge	If you want to get into the canyon faster, this is the shortest hike you can take. This is a moderate hike with a distance of 3.1 miles, which will take you around 2 hours to complete. The path is also nicely maintained. To reach the start of the trail, there's a free shuttle bus.
Trail of Time on the Rim Trail	This is an easy hike for beginners because it's only around 1.5 miles long within the Rim Trail. However, this trail is often crowded, so you need to begin early in the morning. Along the path, you may learn more about the colors and layers of rocks. You can even take your children on this hike because it's family-friendly.
Bright Angel to Indian Garden	This trail is a popular but very challenging hike. With a distance of 8.8 miles, you can complete this hike in around 6 hours. Many hikers even decide to camp at the Indian Garden and return the next day. However, this trail is always packed with people, so starting your hike early is much better.

Trail	Description
North Kaibab to Roaring Springs	This is a challenging trail that is 8.4 miles long and will take you over 4 hours to finish. This trail is popular among experienced hikers and backpackers. Along the path, you'll see the Redwall Limestone cliffs and a waterfall coming out of a spring.
Widforss	This is the longest trail, with a distance of 9.3 miles. It's considered a moderate hike since it will take you about 4 hours to complete. There are trees along the path to protect you from the sun. Most of the trail is level with the ground, making it suitable for beginners and runners.
Cape Royal	This is an easy and family-friendly trail that you can bring your kids to. It's only one mile long, which may take around 20 minutes to finish. The path is mostly paved, so it's very convenient for wheelchair users. However, the trail can be crowded when the North Rim is open.

Since most of these trails are moderate or challenging, you must prepare your body beforehand. You'll also need to wear proper clothing, bring appropriate equipment, and make sure you have enough drinking water. If you hike in the summer, you need to bring a hat, wear sunscreen, and take your sunglasses to protect yourself from the sun.

Taking a River Trip

If you enjoy water activities and wish to explore the Grand Canyon through the Colorado River, you can do a river trip. You'll encounter times of sheer excitement and complete calmness, as well as a sense of community. You will be able to immerse in nature, while at the same time learning everything you need to know about the Grand Canyon and Colorado River's history. Additionally, you'll meet fascinating new people and establish relationships with them.

There are two types of river trips you can take, including a half-day or full-day that can be organized by a park's accommodation and whitewater trips that may last from 3 to 21 days (*Things to do*, 2023). For whitewater trips, you must reserve a spot in advance and apply for a permit. If you go on a tour, you'll be provided with a tour guide who will share their knowledge and experience throughout the trip.

Mule Riding

If you're looking for a more challenging and adventurous experience at the Grand Canyon, you can take a mule ride to explore it. This activity is very unique and unusual since not many places offer mule rides. If you decide to take an overnight trip, you'll travel to the bottom of the canyon and stay at the Phantom Ranch. The Grand Canyon is very breathtaking when you view it from the inside, which makes traveling to the bottom much more rewarding. However, if you don't have the time to stay overnight, you may also take a two-hour ride during the day. But this short trip doesn't take you deep within the canyon but only around the South Rim.

The South Rim mule rides are available to visitors all year round, and reservations can be made 15 months beforehand. It's recommended to reserve a spot months before your trip because the park is so crowded during the summer. To stay at the Phantom Ranch, you'll also need a reservation. Some rules to follow are that all passengers need to be over 9 years old, the weight limit is 200 lbs, and the minimum height is 57 inches (*Mule trips*, 2021).

Visiting Lookout Points

In the South Rim, there are various viewpoints to look over the Grand Canyon from different perspectives. Every one of these locations provides breathtaking scenery, but some are just superior to others. Some have magnificent views, and others are great places to see the sun when it rises and sets. The following is a list of some viewpoints within the Grand Canyon:

Area	Description
Desert View Drive	You can't take the free shuttle bus to get here, so you must drive your own car because it stretches over 25 miles (Julie, 2023a). Desert View, Moran, Shoshone, and Grand View Points are the best viewpoints here.
Grand Canyon Village	To reach this area, you may take the shuttle bus. If you like hiking, you can hike the Rim Trail. The most known lookout points here are Mather, Ooh Aah, Yaki, and Yavapai Points.
Hermit Road	With a distance of 7 miles, there are some popular viewpoints along this road, like Pima, Powell, and Mohave Points. You may also take a shuttle to reach this area.

<table>
<tr><td></td><td>However, if you're visiting in the summer, you can drive your car.</td></tr>
</table>

Please note that some lookout points are very crowded, and if you dislike that, you should find a quieter and more private one.

Riding a Train

If you want to go sightseeing from inside the comfort of a train, you can take a ride on the Grand Canyon Railway. This train transports its passengers from Williams to explore and pass through the breathtaking scenery of the Grand Canyon. Established in 1901, this railway is over 60 miles long and will take around two hours to complete (Kwak-Hefferan, 2012). When you pass the Grand Canyon, you'll also see various wildlife grazing or flying through the sky, like eagles, mule deer, and elk. There are different classes within the train, and the price starts from $29 for children and $65 for adults. In addition, the train will depart from Williams at 9:30 a.m. and from the Grand Canyon at 3:30 p.m., and you must arrive at least 15 minutes before your departure.

Furthermore, it's also essential to dress according to the season you're visiting the Grand Canyon. The weather can change suddenly in the fall and spring months, so it's important to layer your clothing or bring an additional jacket in case the temperature drops on the way.

Taking a Jeep Tour

Another way to explore the Grand Canyon with your family and friends is by taking a Jeep tour. These Jeep tours can be found in the South Rim and West Rim areas. However, since the South Rim is much more popular, there are more options for Jeep tours there. This tour will take you to various hotspots within the Grand Canyon, so you won't have to worry about where to go first. You'll also be provided with a tour guide who will educate you about the Grand Canyon's history, culture, wildlife, and geology. This means that you can ask as many questions as you want about the park.

These tours typically take you around for about two to three hours. You may also choose to ride in the morning or afternoon. If you've decided to take a Jeep tour, you must budget at least $100 for a two-hour ride.

Visiting the Yavapai Museum of Geology

To know more about the history of the Grand Canyon, you can visit the Yavapai Museum of Geology. You'll learn how the canyon was formed and all the rocks within the park because all the exhibits available in the museum are geology-related. The museum also features a large window to look over the Grand Canyon. Moreover, you don't need to pay any money to enter the museum. Some other facilities here are a bookstore, a gift shop, and an amphitheater.

Biking at the Grand Canyon

It's also possible to bike at the Grand Canyon. However, the options are a bit more limited than the other national parks. Mountain bikes are not permitted on the majority of the roads because they're always packed with other vehicles, which can be dangerous for bikers. It's recommended to always wear bright-colored clothes and helmets so that other drivers can notice you right away.

In the South Rim, you're permitted to bike along Hermit Road. From March to October, the road offers a calm and pleasurable biking experience, with only a few buses that drive by occasionally. However, you need to stop on the side of the road when a big vehicle passes to avoid unwanted accidents.

If you want to bike in the North Rim, you need to avoid the Cape Royal area because the roads are very narrow and have low visibility. A great option is to bike from the North Kaibab Trailhead because the trail is open for bikers and even pets (Absolon, 2020). Mountain biking is also allowed in the North Rim, and the park management has opened the Rainbow Rim Trail for mountain bikers, which stretches for over 18 miles (Absolon, 2020). The path has stunning views, and you'll also see different wildlife in their natural habitat.

If you don't have a personal bike, Bright Angel Bicycles in the South Rim region offers bike rentals. It features a wide range of bike options to suit your needs. Not only that, but it also has a cafe offering coffee and baked goods where you can have breakfast before your ride.

Joining a Guided Ranger Program

If you're taking your kids with you and want them to learn more about the Grand Canyon, you may sign up for a program guided by the park rangers. The ranger programs are only available in the South Rim Village, and there are many activities you can join. The programs are divided into two parts, including the ones that are available from Thursday to Monday and the activities open from Friday to Sunday.

Let's take a look at the Thursday through Monday programs:

- **Geology talk:** This program starts at 2 p.m. and lasts for about 30 minutes. You need to go to the Yavapai Museum of Geology to join it. You'll discover the formation history of the Grand Canyon, explained by a park ranger. They'll share why it's so unique and how it can't be found anywhere else. After the talk, most people will go down the Trail of Time since it's not that far from the museum.

- **Critter chat:** This one begins at 11 a.m. and takes less than 30 minutes. It starts at the Grand Canyon Visitor Center. A park ranger will explain the diverse animal populations within the park and how they live and survive in their natural habitats.

- **Ranger's choice:** This program always starts at 3:30 p.m. and also lasts for 30 minutes. You'll be greeted by a park ranger at the Yavapai Museum of Geology. The topic for this talk will change every day, so it will be a surprise every time. Perhaps the park ranger will talk about history, wildlife, or astronomy.

- **Family-friendly program:** It starts at 1:30 p.m. and takes around 30 minutes to finish. This program is made to educate kids or even adults in a fun and entertaining way. The topic will also change every day. Additionally, you have to be at Verkamp's Visitor Center to join it.

Furthermore, here are a couple of programs available from Friday through Sunday:

- **Evening program:** This one will last for about an hour and take place in the evening. However, the exact time and place will change, so you must check the visitor's center for accurate information. Some activities in this program are watching stars, learning about constellations, and seeing a meteor shower.

- **Fossil discovery walk:** It starts early at 9 a.m. and typically lasts for an hour. You'll have to go to the Bright Angel Trailhead to be able to join it. You'll walk along the trail guided by a park ranger to explore and learn more about fossils. There are many fossils found within the Grand Canyon, especially those of marine creatures.

Riding a Helicopter

If you have a little bit more in your budget to spend, you can go on a helicopter ride to look over the stunning landscape of the Grand Canyon. You'll experience what it's like soaring through the sky to watch the Colorado River and other famous attractions within the park. These helicopter rides can be taken from the South Rim, West Rim, and Las Vegas. Many tour companies offer them so you can choose one that suits you. These tours typically last for about 30 minutes, and they cost anywhere from $175 to $500 per person (Tim, 2023). Some known companies for these rides are Maverick, Papillon, and Grand Canyon Helicopters.

Key Takeaways

- Situated in Arizona state, Grand Canyon National Park received its official title as a national park in 1919.

- The Spanish were the first explorers who arrived at the Grand Canyon.

- The most well-known destinations at the Grand Canyon are Mather Point, South Rim, and Desert View Drive.

- Some important details you must know before visiting are its operating seasons and hours, entrance fees and passes, permits, accommodations, and campgrounds.

- There are a lot of fun activities to do in the Grand Canyon, such as hiking, taking a river trip, mule riding, visiting lookout points, riding a train, joining a guided ranger program, and more.

In Chapter 5, you'll find out everything to know about Mount Rainier National Park, from its history and culture to the best activities to do within the park.

Mount Rainier National Park

Did you know that Rainier wasn't the mountain's original name? It was given the name of Tahoma or Tacoma by the Native Americans before the Europeans came across it (*Black to the park*, 2023). However, the name was then changed by British Royal Navy Captain George Vancouver to honor his friend Rear Admiral Peter Rainier in 1792 (*Mount Rainier history*, 2023). He came upon the mountain when he was exploring the area and was amazed by the mountain's breathtaking beauty. However, Peter Rainier never got the chance to visit America and see the mountain named after him in real life.

History and Culture

In order to preserve Mount Rainier and protect the nature surrounding it, Mount Rainier National Park was founded in 1899 (Pletcher, 2023). This park is situated within Washington state in the United States. The mountain peak is covered in ice, and the region surrounding the summit is still surrounded by glaciers. This leads to the park having cool weather even during the summer months. However, the temperature will drop significantly as you go up higher to Mount Rainier's peak.

Furthermore, the national park doesn't only consist of Mount Rainier. The entire park covers 236,381 acres of land, and more than half of them are forested areas (*Black to the park*, 2023). The most common trees inhabiting these forests are western red cedars, pines, mountain hemlocks, and Douglas firs (Pletcher, 2023). Many of these trees grow to become very large, especially in the park's lower-elevation forests.

The park has a very rich human history and culture that dates back over 9,000 years (*Mount Rainier history*, 2023). The Native American people used this area as their main resource to survive. They often hunted wild animals, gathered plants, and built their homes across the region. The most common animal that they hunted were mountain goats, while the plants they would gather and use were cedar bark and huckleberries. If you think about it, it's hard to really call the area a wilderness anymore since it has been touched by human civilization for hundreds of years. Now, the park has become a popular tourist destination, with over two million people visiting each year.

There are some Native American Tribes who called the park their ancestral home. Even to this day, they're still trying to protect and preserve the park by using the knowledge they received from their ancestors. Some of these tribes are Nisqually, Squaxin Island, Cowlitz, Coast Salish, Puyallup, and Yakama (*Mount Rainier history*, 2023).

Now that you know some of the history, you might be wondering what some of the famous attractions to visit at Mount Rainier are. The first one is Paradise Area. Most visitors start their journey of exploring the park from this point because the main visitor center is in the area. It transforms into an excellent location to watch wildflowers blossom during the summer months. In the winter, the area then shifts to become the primary hotspot for skiing and snowshoeing. Additionally, there are stunning meadows and lakes in the area, so you'll keep finding surprises as you explore it.

The second destination is Sunrise Point Overlook. This is a lookout point where you can see the valleys of Mount Rainier. Because it's high up, many visitors choose to hike to reach it. But if you don't feel like hiking, this point can be reached by vehicle. Two known trails lead here, including Sunrise Nature and Sunrise Rim Trails (*Sunrise*, 2021). Since it's very popular, it's often packed with visitors, which makes it hard to get a parking spot.

Moreover, Longmire is also a popular attraction. The entrance to Mount Rainier used to be at Longmire. In 1916, it was the original headquarters of the park before turning into a National Historic District (Julie, 2022). Around the property, you'll find some known hiking trails and hot springs. It's also surrounded by forested areas, which makes it a great attraction if you like spending time in nature. The Longmire building now has become a museum to learn about Mount Rainier's history.

With its various landscapes, Mount Rainier creates different habitats for wildlife. The park is home to a diverse animal population filled with mammals, birds, reptiles, and fish. There are over 300 species of animals inhabiting the park (*Mount Rainier animals*, 2021). The most common mammals to discover here are deer, raccoons, mountain goats, coyotes, mountain lions, bobcats, and bears. Additionally, you'll also see various birds flying over, such as eagles, owls, woodpeckers, bluebirds, jays, and warblers. Meanwhile, some fish and reptiles found here are salmon, trout, snakes, and alligators. This means that Mount Rainier is a great option if you enjoy wildlife viewing.

Basic Information

If you've chosen Mount Rainier National Park to go to on your next trip, there are a few important details to know first. From its opening seasons and hours to its campgrounds, I'll explain everything in this section.

Opening Seasons and Hours

The park can be accessed all year long, and its gate is open 24/7. However, Mount Rainier receives the most visitors in the summer, especially from July to August. This happens because wildflowers will bloom during these two months. Many flock to the park just to see all the different colors of these wildflowers. If you plan to visit the park in the summer, it's recommended to avoid the weekends or holidays since the parking spots are limited. You also should arrive at Mount Rainier early in the morning or late in the afternoon to avoid getting stuck at the entrance.

The park is not too crowded during the fall and winter seasons. But there might be some facilities or roads that are closed, so you must check for accurate information beforehand. The weather may also change drastically during these seasons, so you need to prepare yourself.

Furthermore, the opening hours depend on the visitor center you visit. There are four different visitor centers within the park, as follows:

1. **Ohanapecosh Visitor Center:** 9 a.m. to 5 p.m.

2. **Longmire Museum:** 9 a.m. to 4:30 p.m.

3. **Sunrise Visitor Center:** 9 a.m. to 5 p.m.

4. **Henry M. Jackson Memorial at Paradise:** 9 a.m. to 5:30 p.m.

Please note that these are the normal opening hours for the visitor centers, and you must check online before visiting. Moreover, these visitor centers are mostly open from June to September.

Entrance Fees and Passes

In order to enter Mount Rainier, you need to get a park pass and pay a fee. The standard entrance fee costs around $15–$30 per person or vehicle, which is valid for seven days. Meanwhile, the annual entrance fee is priced at $55 per person, which is cheaper than the other national parks in previous chapters. To get a pass, you can purchase them at the entrance during the day because there's a staff working. However, if you plan to enter late in the day, you'll need to buy your pass online.

Permits

Depending on what kind of activity you do at Mount Rainier, you may need to apply for a permit. Let's take a look at some activities that require one so that you don't make the mistake of not having it while visiting:

- **Wilderness permit:** This one is required when you plan to stay overnight in the backcountry areas of Mount Rainier. You should apply for this permit during the summer.

- **Climbing permit:** You need to have a permit if you wish to visit one of the glaciers and climb over 10,000 feet (*Mount Rainier permits and reservations*, 2023).

- **Commercial use authorizations:** This is needed for all commercial activities held within the park, like photography classes or guided bike tours.

- **Special use permits:** Many visitors come to Mount Rainier for special occasions because of its stunning environment. Some events that need a permit are wedding ceremonies, video filming, military activities, school trips, and group recreation.

Accommodations

Are you interested in staying overnight inside or near the Mount Rainier area? There are a couple of options to consider. In this section, I'll let you know about the lodges within the park and some accommodations nearby.

Places to Stay Within Mount Rainier Area

The park has two lodging options situated inside. This means that you don't have many options, so most visitors reserve a room months in advance. Here are the options:

- **Paradise Inn:** Designed with a rustic style, this accommodation opened its doors in 1916 (*Mount Rainier lodging*, 2023). However, it's only available for booking from May to October. It offers over 100 rooms and some other facilities like a cafe, gift shop, and post office.

- **National Park Inn:** This accommodation is open all year long. However, it's very limited since it only has 25 rooms. The facilities are also very basic, such as a cleaning service, dining room, and small store.

Places to Stay Near the Park

Since the options are very limited inside the park, most visitors stay the night at one of the accommodations nearby. The following are some other lodges close to it:

- **Mineral Lake Lodge:** Situated only around 20 minutes away from the park, this is a known accommodation among visitors. It's also located next to Mineral Lake if you enjoy water activities. Not only that, but it also offers some facilities like picnic areas, campfire spots, and a free breakfast.

- **Wilderness Edge Cabin:** If you enjoy sleeping at a place surrounded by trees, this is perfect for you. Moreover, it's only around four miles from the park entrance. Some facilities it offers are a kitchen, picnic tables, and a fireplace.

- **Rainier Cottages:** This one is a more luxurious accommodation because every cottage has its own hot tub. It only has 10 cottages available, so you need to reserve it in advance. Additionally, it only takes five minutes to reach the park entrance. A few other amenities it offers are a wood stove, kitchen, and a campfire.

- **Nisqually Lodge:** This accommodation offers hotel rooms with modern style. It has over 20 rooms for its guests with private bathrooms and TVs. Moreover, you'll get breakfast every day while staying here.

- **Three Bears Lodge:** This is also a lodge surrounded by trees that will help you enjoy nature. Not only that, but it's also situated minutes away from the park entrance. Since this is a big cabin that can fit eight people, it's perfect for those coming with their family or friends.

- **Whittakers Bunkhouse:** Just like the name, this property was originally a bunkhouse before turning into a lodge. It offers 18 different rooms with private bathrooms. There are also dormitories with bunk beds if that's your preference. Many hikers and climbers choose this accommodation before visiting the park.

Picnic Areas

If you bring your children to Mount Rainier, you can take them to a picnic area to enjoy the view. The best season for a picnic is in the summer months when you can see the wildflowers blooming and look at the mountain views. The park has several picnic sites spread over various areas. Additionally, they're typically equipped with picnic tables. Are you ready for a picnic? Prepare your lunch and cold beverages. After that, you can pick one of these picnic areas:

- **Cougar Rock:** If you'd like a tranquil setting for your picnic, Cougar Rock is located in a forested area of Mount Rainier. This place will allow you to escape the city's chaotic life.

- **White River:** Since it's located near some trailheads, it is often a stopping point for hikers before they start their hikes.

- **Ohanapecosh:** This one is also situated in a quiet forested area close to the Ohanapecosh River. You can look over the river while having a picnic here.

- **Sunrise:** This is the most popular picnic area because you can view the mountain while enjoying your lunch. Along the way, you'll also see wildflower meadows.

- **Paradise:** Not only does it have picnic tables, but this picnic site also provides grills for visitors. When the weather is clear, you'll be able to see the mountain's breathtaking view.

- **Box Canyon:** This area is popular for those who explore Mount Rainier with their vehicle. It provides visitors with a picnic site and restroom when they stop by.

Campgrounds

If you wish to stay the night out in nature, you can reserve a campsite at one of the park's campgrounds. Mount Rainier offers its visitors three different campgrounds with hundreds of campsites. Here's a list of these campgrounds along with their individual and group prices:

Campground	Price (Nightly)
Ohanapecosh	Individual: $20 Group: $60
Cougar Rock	Individual: $20 Group: $60
White River	Individual: $20 Group: No group campsites available

Please note that these are the campgrounds' current costs, and you must check for accurate prices online before your visit. Ohanapecosh and Cougar Rock Campgrounds can be booked online via Recreation.gov. However, White River Campground can only be reserved on-site.

Furthermore, there are some rules to follow at these campgrounds. First, it's prohibited to sleep in your car. After that, you're only allowed to park at the parking lot provided by the park. Additionally, you can't camp in the park for more than two weeks at a time and no more than four weeks in a year.

Summer Activities

During the summer months, Mount Rainier is always packed with tourists from all over the country. This is because there are a lot of activities you can do within the vast land of the park. Let's explore each of them so that you can plan your vacation easily.

Hiking a Trail

Mount Rainier has become a wonderland for hikers since it provides around 260 miles of well-maintained hiking trails (*Day hiking at Mount Rainier*, 2023). These trails will take you to remote places within the park, where you can find some quiet and tranquility. Along the way, you'll pass through stunning places like meadows, rivers, glaciers, and lakes. At Mount Rainier, there are many trails with various distances and difficulties. In this section, I'll lay out everything to know about them.

Longmire Trails

Trail	Description
Rampart Ridge	Situated within the Longmire area, this moderate trail is almost 5 miles for a round trip. This means that it will take you around 2 to 3 hours to complete, depending on your speed. Along the path, you'll pass through some valleys where you can see the mountain views. However, you're not allowed to

	bring a pet here.
Trail of the Shadows	This is a short hike with moderate difficulty. With a distance of 0.4 miles, you can finish it in under 20 minutes. This trail is made for those who like solitude because it's surrounded by trees.
Twin Firs Loop	This is an easy and short hike that's great to see wildlife. It's only a 0.7-mile round trip, which will take you around 15 to 20 minutes to finish. Along the way, you'll see the forests and meadows and all the animals going about their day.

Ohanapecosh Trails

Trail	Description
Box Canyon Loop	This trail is only 0.5 miles roundtrip and is considered an easy one. It's also family-friendly, so you can bring your kids on this hike. Most people can finish it in under 15 minutes.
Silver Falls Loop	With a distance of 3 miles, this loop trail can be done in an hour or two. This is an easy hike passing through the Silver Falls. If you plan to stay at Paradise Inn, this is the closest hiking to it.

Grove of the Patriarchs	This trail passes through the forests surrounded by cedar and Douglas fir trees. It's around 1.3 miles long, and it will take an hour to complete. However, due to significant damage from flooding, it's currently unavailable to visitors until the bridge can be repaired.
Hot Springs	This is an easy hike that takes under 30 minutes to finish. This is also great for those who enjoy solitude because the trail is shaded by huge trees. It's a very short hike with 0.5 miles in distance.

Carbon River and Mowich Trails

Trail	Description
Tolmie Peak	This 6.5-mile loop trail can be finished in around 3 to 4 hours. The moderate hike passes through the forests and meadows and takes you to Tolmie Peak. It's important to stay walking on the path to avoid damaging the meadows.
Old Mine	This moderate loop trail is almost 3 miles long and can be finished in an hour or two. You'll walk along the forested area that leads to an old mine entrance.

Green Lake	This trail has a distance of 9 miles that may take you over four hours to complete. You'll walk in the forested areas to reach Green Lake and view Ranger Falls.
Chenuis Falls	This is a moderate and long hike that you can complete in around 2 to 3 hours. With a distance of 7.9 miles, this trail will take you to see the view of Chenuis Falls.
Carbon River Rain Forest Nature	This is an easy and short hike that you can finish in under 20 minutes. It's a very popular trail, so you'll meet many hikers or runners along the path.

Paradise Trails

Trail	**Description**
Skyline to Myrtle Falls	From Skyline trail, you can arrive at Myrtle Falls in under 40 minutes. This is a moderate hike equipped with paved trails, making it convenient. Along the path, you'll also experience the view of Mount Rainier.
Nisqually Vista	This one is a family-friendly hike because you'll only pass the meadows to see the mountain views. With a distance of 1.2

	miles, it can be completed in under an hour.
Bench and Snow Lakes	Situated close to Paradise Inn, this trail is only 2.5 miles long, which you can complete in an hour or two. On the way, you'll enjoy the views of two lakes and see wildflower meadows. However, this is a moderate hike since some areas have steep paths.

Paradise Trails

Trail	Description
Glacier Basin	This is the best trail to see wildflowers blooming in the summer. With a distance of 7 miles, this moderate hike can be finished in around 4 to 5 hours. You'll pass through the meadows and mountainous areas where you can see mountain goats.
Shadow Lakes	This trail is great for families with kids. It's only around 3 miles roundtrip, which you can complete in an hour or two. Along the path, you'll find meadows and look over the mountain.
Nache Peak Loop	This loop trail is 3.5 miles long

	and may take you two hours to finish. When the fall season arrives, you'll find huckleberries along the way. Additionally, this moderate trail offers stunning views of Mount Rainier.
Dege Peak through Sourdough Ridge	To reach Dege Peak, you'll need around 2 hours through Sourdough Ridge. This moderate hike also offers great views of Mount Rainier, Mount Adams, and Glacier Peak (*Day hiking at Mount Rainier*, 2023).

Hiking Regulations at Mount Rainier

Before hiking one of the trails above, you must pay attention to the regulations enforced by the park.

- Pets are not allowed on any of the trails.

- Bikes are prohibited from entering the hiking trails.

- Visitors can't have more than 12 individuals in their hiking groups.

- Wildflower meadows need to be preserved, so visitors must refrain from stomping over them.

- It's prohibited to feed wild animals because human food might harm them.

Climbing and Mountaineering

Climbing has become a popular activity among visitors at the park. Of course, this happens because the main thing that attracts people is Mount Rainier. Filled with various glaciers and a peak covered in ice, it offers a challenge to climbers. Every year, thousands of climbers flock to the park just to successfully reach the peak of Mount Rainier. The park management provides four major trailheads when traveling up the mountain, including the Westside Road, Paradise, Mowich Lake, and White River areas (*Mount Rainier climbing*, 2023). You'll need to research each of these trails to see which one fits you best.

There is a fee you need to pay before you can get a climbing permit. Everyone needs to pay an annual climbing fee of $65 prior to visiting the park through pay.gov/public/form/start/79997374 (*Mount Rainier climbing*, 2023). You can apply for a climbing permit at one of the park's ranger stations.

Furthermore, the way to the mountain peak is very steep, which makes it dangerous if your body is not in a healthy condition. All climbers need to be in great physical condition before climbing. Not only that, but you'll also have to be well-prepared. You must make sure you have the proper equipment for your safety. The temperature will drop drastically as you go up, so you need to wear layers of thick clothing to avoid hypothermia.

If you don't want to climb independently, you may also hire a guide to direct you or join a climbing tour. There are some companies that offer guides inside the park, such as Rainier Mountaineering, Inc. and Alpine Ascents International. You can visit their websites for more information.

Watching Wildflowers

Mount Rainier is known for its wildflower meadows. Every summer, many visitors visit the park just to see the beautiful wildflowers bloom. However, the bloom relies on the weather, so no one can predict it accurately. Currently, these wildflowers often start to bloom in July and persist through August. This means that you must always check for accurate information if you plan to see the wildflowers.

The most important thing to note when watching these wildflowers is to not pick them in order to preserve their beauty. You must always stay on the designated pathways to avoid stomping on or damaging them as well. Moreover, there are some hotspots to discover wildflowers, as follows:

- **Mowich Lake:** Colorful wildflower meadows surround the lake. There are some trails along the lake where you can walk to see the flowers. Two common flowers here are Lewis' monkeyflower and mountain bog gentian.

- **Paradise:** When the wildflowers bloom, this area is filled with various colors. To view the flowers, the meadows are surrounded by different trails to walk along with your family. Some of the flowers blooming here are pearly everlasting, Lewis' monkeyflower, and rosy spirea.

- **Sunrise:** This area also has some wildflower meadows surrounding it. It's a popular spot for hikers because it's much higher up than Paradise. A few flower species found here are Sitka valerian, Cascade aster, and paintbrush.

Biking at Mount Rainier

Biking is also a great activity to do when visiting Mount Rainier. However, biking within the park can be challenging since the roads pass through the forests, which may be steep, rocky, or slippery. Although it's challenging, biking at Mount Rainier is rewarding because you'll experience the scenic and stunning views of the park.

The best months to bike here are September and October because the fall season begins, so there are fewer cars on the roads. Additionally, you'll also see the beautiful colors of fall throughout the forested areas and meadows. But you must know that during this season, there are some roads and facilities that are closed until spring or summer. This means that you need to check the road status before biking. Some of the best areas for biking are Carbon River Road, Greenwood Lake, and Osborne Mountain.

Furthermore, visitors are allowed to bike on the park's roads since there are no specific bike trails. However, hiking trails are off-limits to avoid disturbing the hikers. To keep yourself safe, you must always wear a bright-colored helmet so that others can see you right away. Additionally, it is crucial to communicate your intentions to other drivers by using hand gestures. If you plan to bike to a high-elevation area, you need to wear proper clothing because the temperature may drop dramatically. When you go downhill, it's also crucial to keep a safe distance from other bikers to prevent an accident. Biking equipment and facilities within or around the park are limited, so you must bring your own repair kit.

Fishing

If you enjoy fishing with a view, Mount Rainier is the perfect place for this activity. The park is also home to various fish species, which makes it a great destination for fishing. Several common fish species here are trout, salmon, and whitefish. While offering recreational options for visitors, the park is also committed to the preservation of the water ecosystems and fish species (*Fishing and boating*, 2021). If you decide to fish here, you don't have to get a fishing license. But if you wish to catch steelhead trout or salmon, you'll have to apply for the Washington State catch record (*Fishing and boating*, 2021).

Mount Rainier offers various hotspots for fishing, including rivers, lakes, and streams. Depending on your preference, you may choose one or more destinations for your next fishing trip. Some of the best spots known to visitors are the Nisqually River, Mowich Lake, Butter Creek, Carbon River, and Dog Lake. However, each place has its own rules that you must check before fishing.

Junior Ranger Program

To begin exploring Mount Rainier, you can join the junior ranger activity. This program is made for those who wish to protect while also learning about the park. The park provides a booklet for you to fill out when exploring various attractions of Mount Rainier. This booklet can be found in some visitor centers, including the Ohanapecosh, Sunrise, and Longmire areas. This activity is not just for kids, adults can do it as well. After finishing the booklet, you can hand it over to the staff at the visitor center to get a badge for becoming a junior ranger. This badge is a good souvenir to remind you of your visit to the park.

The booklet can be filled out in less than an hour, so it won't take up too much time. It's available all year long, depending on the visitor centers' opening hours. There is also a fee that you need to pay to get the booklet.

Wildlife Viewing

Mount Rainier is inhabited by various animal populations, which makes it a great destination for wildlife viewing. As previously mentioned, there are over 300 species of wildlife residing within the park, including mountain lions, black bears, elk, and mountain goats. Animals are unpredictable, so there are no promises that you'll see what you want. However, here is a list of popular spots for wildlife viewing:

- **Sunrise:** If you walk along the trails in the Sunrise area, you'll pass through various meadows to reach high-elevation areas. As you go up the mountain, you'll see mountain goats with their herd and squirrels jumping from tree to tree. Not only that, but you may also sometimes see black bears, although they like hiding from humans.

- **Paradise:** Since this area consists of meadows and mountains, you'll see a variety of wildlife in their natural habitat. The most common animals seen here are marmots and butterflies. Red foxes are also often seen in the picnic areas of Paradise.

- **Longmire:** This area is mostly surrounded by forests, and you'll also discover red foxes lurking around. In a higher elevation area, you may see mountain goats going about their day.

Safety Measures

When watching wildlife, there are some safety measures to protect yourself and the animals. What are they?

- You're not allowed to feed the animals, and you'll get fined if someone finds out.

- It's prohibited to leave your food out in the open because predators might approach it.

- When you see a mountain lion, you shouldn't run but stick with your group and back away slowly.

- If a predator like a black bear or mountain lion approaches you, you need to make yourself look big by shouting loudly or throwing something at them.

Winter Activities

If you think there's nothing to do during the winter at Mount Rainier, then you're mistaken. Although your options are limited, there are still a couple of activities to do, from skiing to camping. Let's take a look at some of the winter activities at the park.

Skiing and Snowboarding

Whether you want to ski or snowboard at Mount Rainier, they're both possible during the winter. However, the park only allows these activities when at least five feet of snow covers the ground (*Winter recreation*, 2023). This regulation is made to ensure the preservation of vegetation under it. Mount Rainier offers various trails for skiing and snowboarding, including Mount Rainier Standard Summit Route, Panorama Point through Skyline Trail, and Emerald Ridge Trail. For more information about these activities, you can visit the visitor's center.

Camping in the Winter

During the winter months, camping is allowed in some areas of Mount Rainier. However, just like skiing and snowboarding, snow has to reach a depth of five feet in the Paradise area. But other areas like Reflection Lakes or Mazama Ridge only need two feet of snow (*Winter recreation*, 2023). If you plan to winter camp, obtaining a wilderness permit in advance is a must because these areas are not designated campgrounds. Additionally, you can only get this permit from Longmire Museum.

Snowmobiling

If you enjoy snowmobiling, the park offers a designated trail for this activity on Westside Road and Cougar Rock areas. The Westside Road stretches over six miles, which is closed to other vehicles visiting the park (*Winter recreation*, 2023). Moreover, there are loop trails within the Cougar Rock area for snowmobiling. A couple of guided tours are offered for this activity. Typically, these tours will take you around for an hour or two.

Sledding

In the winter, the roads in the Paradise area are close to vehicles. The park then turns this area into a sledding destination each year. Sledding is only allowed in Paradise because other areas are not as safe. If you like sledding, you may visit Mount Rainier from December to March. Furthermore, visitors are not allowed to go out of the designated area in case unwanted accidents happen. It's also important to wear proper equipment during the activity.

Snowshoeing

Mount Rainier also offers guided tours with park rangers for those who wish to snowshoe. Through this tour, you'll find out more about the park's wildlife and vegetation. These tours are open from December to March and are available on Saturdays and Sundays (*Winter recreation*, 2023). However, you can't make a reservation online because you may only sign up at the Jackson Visitor Center. In addition, you must arrive at least an hour before the tour begins. Lastly, these tours usually only take two hours to finish.

Key Takeaways

- Mount Rainier National Park is situated in Washington State and began its operations in 1899.

- Mount Rainier is a mountain that's covered in ice and surrounded by glaciers.

- There are some famous attractions at the park, such as the Paradise area, Sunrise Point Overlook, and Longmire.

- When organizing your itinerary, you need to know some essential information, from its opening hours and seasons to its picnic areas and campgrounds.

- In the summer, several activities to do are hiking, climbing, watching wildflowers, biking, fishing, and more.

- During the winter, there are also a few fun activities available, such as skiing and snowboarding, camping, snowmobiling, snowshoeing, and sledding.

In the next chapter, we will talk more about Rocky Mountain National Park. You'll figure out the information to know before visiting the park.

Chapter 6:

Rocky Mountain National Park

Rocky Mountain National Park is ranked among the highest ones in the US due to its elevation, which ranges from 7,860 to 14,259 feet (*Natural features & ecosystems*, 2018). Climbing its peaks will surely make you feel that you're standing on the same level as the sky. Additionally, it's hardly surprising that Rocky Mountain is known across the world for its breathtaking views that take you to the top of the world.

History and Culture

Situated in Colorado, Rocky Mountain National Park was founded in 1915 (Zelazko, 2023). With an area that covers over 400 square miles, the land is filled with valleys, mountain peaks, meadows, and forests (*History of Rocky Mountain National Park*, 2023). The park is full of various mountains that shape the range. This then creates magnificent views when the sky is clear. There are over 60 mountain peaks within the park that are higher than 21,000 feet (*Natural features & ecosystems*, 2018).

About 11,000 years ago, people started exploring these mountainous areas for the first time. These earliest inhabitants of the area came from distant old civilizations because not many things are known about them, and they're frequently called Paleo-Indians (*Human history of Rocky Mountain National Park*, 2023). Because they were nomadic, they only passed through the area occasionally. They used the land to hunt and gather plants to survive. However, there were two known Native American tribes who lived there until the Europeans set their sights on the land. These tribes were the Ute and Arapaho people, who were displaced by the settlers around 150 years ago (*Human history of Rocky*

Mountain National Park, 2023). Because of this, they were forced to move to reservations made for Native American people.

Beyond its history, Rocky Mountain National Park is home to various stunning attractions within its vast land. The first famous destination known to visitors is Trail Ridge Road. This road offers different spots to look over the mountains and valleys. Most visitors hike and stop at viewpoints along the way to see the scenic views of the Rocky Mountains. Not only that, but you can also experience wildlife viewing along the road because the area is home to various animal populations.

The second destination is Estes Park. Visitors often use the downtown area of this park as their base. When exploring the Rocky Mountains, you'll need a place to stay the night, and this area offers various accommodations. Estes Park is also filled with other things like gift shops, restaurants, and bars. This means that you'll have activities to entertain you even in the evenings. Moreover, the area has views of the mountainous areas, which makes it seem like a magical place.

Another known attraction is Bear Lake. This lake is popular during fall because visitors may see the trees changing colors from green to red and orange. The best way to enjoy the lake views is to walk along the trail surrounding it. You don't need to worry if you don't hike regularly because the trail is only a mile long, which means that everyone can do it. Additionally, you'll also see the views of Hallett Peak from the lake area.

Furthermore, the park is home to diverse wildlife populations. From mammals to reptiles, over 350 species inhabit Rocky Mountain National Park (*Ecology of Rocky Mountain National Park*, 2023). Some animals that can be found here are moose, mule deer, Clark's nutcracker, bighorn sheep, Boreal toad, and black bears. Since there are a variety of animals roaming the park, it has become a great place for wildlife viewing as well.

Basic Information

As you prepare for your visit to Rocky Mountain National Park, you must know all the basic information first. From its operating seasons and hours to the best accommodations and campgrounds, I'll explain everything in this section.

Operating Seasons and Hours

No matter what day you plan to visit the park, it opens its doors to visitors all year long and 24 hours each day. However, there might be days that it's closed, depending on the weather. Many people organize their trips in the summer and fall, so the park will be packed with visitors. You should come earlier or later in the day to prevent getting stuck in traffic.

The park also provides several visitor centers where you can get your information. They also have various opening hours, as follows:

- **Sheep Lakes Information Station:** 9:30 a.m. to 4:30 p.m.

- **Beaver Meadows Visitor Center:** 9:00 a.m. to 6:00 p.m. (summer) and 9:00 a.m. to 4:30 p.m. (spring)

- **Kawuneeche Visitor Center:** 9 a.m. to 5 p.m. (summer)

- **Holzwarth Historic Site:** 9:30 a.m. to 2:30 p.m. (summer)

- **Moraine Park Discovery Center:** 9 a.m. to 4:30 p.m

- **Alpine Visitor Center:** 9:30 a.m. to 5 p.m.

- **Fall River Visitor Center:** 9 a.m. to 5 p.m. (summer)

Please take note that these are the regular hours of operation. You must check for more accurate information on the National Park

Service website because they might close or change hours during the holidays or certain seasons.

Fees and Passes

To enter Rocky Mountain, you'll need to get a pass and pay an entrance fee—the standard entrance fee ranges from $15 to $35 per person or vehicle. Moreover, the annual pass is priced at $70, which you may use for multiple entries within a year. You can access the park through four entrances within the Wild Basin, Beaver Meadows, Grand Lake, and Fall River areas (Peglar, 2023a). However, it's important to note that the park has switched to cashless transactions for all purchases at entries and campgrounds starting June 2023. Another thing the park implemented is that you will need to get a Timed Entry Permit Reservation along with the park pass before entering from May 26 through October 22, 2023 (*Rocky Mountain fees and passes*, 2023).

Permits

Park passes are required for some areas and activities in the park. Permits, just like passes, have particular and special purposes. If you would like to use the park for certain activities, a specific park permit needs to be obtained beforehand. Some activities requiring a permit are wedding ceremonies, church services, photoshoots, public assemblies, special events, filming, and commercial activities.

Accommodations

If your vacation will last for days, you'll have to get yourself a suitable accommodation to make it more memorable. However, no hotels or other accommodations are available within the park. This means that you'll need to get a room in one of the areas nearby. The known areas among visitors are Estes Park and Grand Lake. These communities offer various accommodations along with other facilities like restaurants, bars, shops, and so on. In this section, I'll let you know the best accommodations that you can access in these areas.

Estes Park

This area is known as the gateway to the park. Each year, millions of visitors use it as their home base when exploring the Rocky Mountains. However, there are so many accommodations available. If you're confused about which to choose, here are some of the best ones:

- **Rams Horn Village Resort:** This resort is an excellent choice if you enjoy a luxurious stay. It offers luxury cabins, which makes it the perfect place for those visiting with their families. The best amenity here is their heated pool overlooking the forested areas.

- **The Maxwell Inn:** If you're on a budget, this accommodation offers affordable rooms for its guests. It has all the basic amenities of a hotel, such as complimentary breakfast, TVs, and private bathrooms. However, pets are not allowed to enter the property.

- **Hotel Estes:** This one is another family-friendly accommodation because it provides some suites for families. Not only that, but it also offers various amenities like an outdoor swimming pool, a complimentary breakfast, and picnic areas.

Grand Lake Colorado

If you wish to stay at a place where you can also view the Rocky Mountains, the Grand Lake area is the perfect destination for that. The area even has a lake and forested areas surrounding it. Here is a list of the best accommodations in the area:

- **Spirit Lake Lodge:** Situated in the downtown area of Grand Lake, this lodge is very convenient. It offers hot tubs, rooms with fireplaces, and free parking spots. Additionally, it's pet-friendly, so you can bring your fur friend while staying here.

- **Grand Lake Lodge:** This rustic-style lodge is also a popular place to stay in the area. It offers comfortable rooms and a communal deck where guests can overlook the lake and mountainous area.

- **Western Riviera Lakeside Lodging:** Located close to the lake, this accommodation provides many water activities for its guests. It offers various types of accommodations, from standard motel rooms to lake and tree houses.

Campgrounds

If you wish to stay within the park area, you may opt for camping. The park offers some campgrounds with various campsites for visitors. To get a campsite, you must reserve a spot in advance at Recreation.gov. The following is the list of campgrounds along with their costs:

Campground	Price (Nightly)
Timber Creek	$35
Aspenglen	$35
Moraine Park	$35
Glacier Basin	$35–$70

Please note that these are the current nightly rates of these campgrounds; you must check online for accurate prices prior to booking.

Things to Do

There are a lot of activities to do within Rocky Mountain National Park. Have you decided on which ones to write down on your itinerary? If not, here are some of the best activities to do while visiting the park.

Hiking

The park is surrounded by various beautiful places, from lakes to waterfalls to mountain peaks. If you like to hike, it provides visitors with different hiking trails to choose from. In this section, I'll list the best trails along with their distances, durations, and difficulties.

Waterfall Trails

Trail	Description
Chasm Falls	Through Old Fall River Road, you'll walk along a 4.7-mile loop trail. Typically, hikers would finish this hike in around 2 hours. Along the way, you'll see forested areas and mountain views.
Adams Falls	This short hike is only 0.8 miles in distance. It's an easy trail for families. Normally, it takes less than 30 minutes to finish. Along the path, you'll pass through meadows and forests.

Granite Falls	To reach Granite Falls, you'll need to hike 5.2 miles one way. This is a moderate hike that'll take you around 2 to 3 hours to complete. You'll walk through the meadows and forests, which means that you might see various wildlife.
Cascade Falls	This moderate hike is only 3.5 miles in distance, which may take less than an hour to finish. You'll walk along an open meadow and experience the views of the mountains.
Alberta Falls	This loop trail is only 1.6 miles long and can be completed in around 40 minutes. This area is known for horseback riding in the summer and snowshoeing during the winter.

Lake Trails

Trail	Description
Cub Lake Loop	This moderate loop trail is 6 miles in distance and can be finished in 2 or 3 hours. It's known for its beautiful meadows and forests where you can view wildlife.
Mills Lake	With a distance of 5 miles, you can complete this hike in around

	two hours. This trail is marked well so that you may navigate the area easily. Not only for hiking, but the lake is also great for fishing.
Bear Lake	This easy hike is 0.5 miles for a round trip that'll take you around 15 to 20 minutes to finish. The roads are mostly paved, which makes it convenient for wheelchair users.
Sprague Lake Loop	Only 0.5 miles long, this easy loop pathway may be finished within 20 minutes. If you're with your kids, you can take them for a walk here to see the beautiful lake and mountain views.
Lake Haiyaha	For a round trip, this hike is only 4 miles long. Most people can complete the hike in a little over two hours. This trail is known for its lake views because you'll also see Nymph and Bear Lakes.
Dream Lake	The loop trail is around 2.2 miles long and can be finished in around an hour. This moderate hike has stunning views of the forests and Nymph Lake on its way.
Ypsilon Lake	This difficult trail is around 4 miles long, and you may complete

	it in 5 to 6 hours. The terrain is challenging because you'll have to walk along rocky paths. However, it can be very rewarding since you'll view various mountain peaks.
Gem Lake	This loop trail is around 3.5 miles long and can be completed in under an hour. You'll walk along the stream and pass through the beautiful forests. From this trail, you may also see Longs Peak and Estes Park.
Odessa Lake	This moderate hike is almost 9 miles long, and you can finish it in 4 to 5 hours. You'll hike through the thick pine forests to reach Odessa Lake, where you're allowed to fish.
Chasm Lake	For a round trip, this hike is over 8 miles long. This challenging trail can be completed in 5 to 6 hours. You'll have to climb and pass through rocky pathways to reach the lake. This means your body needs to be in a healthy condition to take on this hike.
The Loch	This moderate is over 6 miles long with a duration of around 2 to 3 hours. Along the path, you'll pass Alberta Falls and also view the Continental Divide. However, it's

	not recommended if you have heart issues since you may need to climb in some areas.
The Pool	To reach the Pool, you'll hike along the Big Thompson River. With a distance of around 3 miles, you can complete it in an hour. It's also considered an easy route since the pathways only pass through the meadows and forests.
Fern Lake	This loop trail is almost 8 miles and can be completed in around 4 to 5 hours. This moderate hike takes you along the Big Thompson River and passes through Fern Falls. Most visitors would stop by to fish in the river before continuing their hike.
East Shore	For a round trip, you must hike over 5 miles. This easy trail takes you along the East Shore and offers views of the mountain peaks in the distance. Along the way, you may also find the chance to watch wildlife.
Bierstadt Lake	This moderate hike is only around 3 miles long for a round trip. You may finish it in under two hours, depending on your speed. Along the path, you can view the Continental Divide and various mountain peaks. However, you

	need to be careful since there might be slippery paths during the rainy season.

Summit Trails

Trail	Description
Deer Mountain	With a distance of 6 miles, this loop trail can be finished in around 3 hours. Not only for hiking, but it is also known for running. Although it's a mountain hike, you'll also pass through some meadows on the way.
Twin Sisters Summit	This one is difficult because you'll have to hike 7.4 miles out and back. However, the views from the trail are amazing since you'll get to see the mountains and pass through the forests.
Flattop Mountain	This difficult and long hike is typically taken by experienced hikers. You need to be fit to take on this 8.8-mile loop trail. However, it's very rewarding because you'll get to experience the entire park's views.
Estes Cone	This challenging hike is over 6 miles for a round trip, which may take around 4 hours to complete.

	Since you'll hike to a higher elevation area, it's not recommended if you have heart or respiratory conditions.

Please note that before hiking, you need to make sure that your body is in good condition to avoid getting hurt. Additionally, the weather might change drastically within the park, so you must bring extra clothing and proper equipment for hiking.

Taking a Drive

The park has a fantastic road system if you want to drive and take in the Rocky Mountain scenery. There are various paved roads in different areas of the park, depending on what you'd like to see. These roads will lead you past the forested areas to the meadows as well as along the lakes and rivers. There are even roads that take you high up the mountains with an elevation of over 12,000 feet (*Scenic drives*, 2021). Not many national parks in the country provide these types of scenic driving experiences.

Since there are many roads to choose from, let's take a look at some of the best ones for a scenic drive:

- **Bear Lake Road:** The head start of this road can be taken after you enter from the Beaver Meadows Entrance. Through this road, you'll drive along forests, where you can see elk or deer wandering in the area. You'll also pass through the Big Thompson River and watch other visitors fish.

- **Trail Ridge Road:** This is the road that takes you high up to an elevation of over 12,000 feet (*Scenic drives*, 2021). This drive allows you to overlook the stunning mountains and valleys. However, the road is closed during the winter since the weather can be dangerous.

- **Devil's Gulch:** From this road, you'll experience the beautiful views of Estes Park and Longs Peak (*Devil's Gulch scenic drive*,

2023). Even though this is a short drive, you may also see the mountains and open meadows on the way.

- **Highway 7:** Although this road is not within the park, it provides a scenic overview of the Rocky Mountains. This road starts from Estes Park and passes through the valley to climb up. Visitors typically stop by on the side of the road to watch the views.

Wildlife Watching and Photography

Rocky Mountain National Park has become a famous place for wildlife viewing throughout the years. Thousands of visitors choose to watch the wildlife here each year. From elk to bighorn sheep, there are a lot of wild animals to see in their natural habitats. However, you must not feed the animals no matter what because human food might make them sick. Some of the best spots for wildlife viewing are Moraine Park, Kawuneeche Valley, Old Fall River Road, Sheep Lakes, and Holzwarth Meadow (Pietrzak, 2023).

If you've decided to watch wildlife, here are a couple of tips to consider:

- The best time to see bighorn sheep is around May to August.

- To see elk, you can visit the place where the forests and meadows connect.

- Mule deer are all over the park, especially in the forested areas far from the mountain peaks.

- If you enjoy birdwatching, you may visit Trail Ridge Road to see Steller's jays and prairie falcons.

- Always bring your binoculars to get a closer view of the animals.

When wildlife watching, you might also want to take pictures of them. If you're a photographer, the following are also several tips to follow:

- The best hours to take pictures are dusk or dawn because of the great lighting.

- It's important to talk quietly to avoid scaring the animals.

- You need to maintain a safe distance to prevent getting attacked by predators.

- If you're in the forest, you can find a bush or tree to hide yourself.

- You may zoom your camera to see the animal closer.

Picnicking

If you want to sit around and relax with your family while enjoying the views, picnicking is a great idea. Rocky Mountain National Park offers over 20 picnic areas spread across the park, and they're available all year long. None of these picnic areas require a reservation. In the eastern part of the park, the best picnic spots are in Hidden Valley, Lily Lake, Beaver Meadows, and Hollowell Park. In the western part, the known ones are Harbison Meadow, Lake Irene, Beaver Creek, and Holzwarth Historic Site.

When picnicking in one of these areas, there are some details you need to know beforehand, as follows:

- The picnic areas are equipped with picnic tables.

- Pets are allowed into the picnic areas, but they need to be on a leash.

- It's prohibited to bring horses or other livestock.

- You may make campfires in the picnic areas, but you're not allowed to collect firewood from the park (which means you need to bring your own).

- It's allowed to use portable grills to cook or heat your food while picnicking.

Guided Ranger Activities

The park also offers different ranger programs where you can talk and walk around guided by park rangers. These activities are free of charge and open to all visitors. There are over 15 programs that you can join. To get more information about them, you need to visit a visitor center to learn the details.

On the east side, the park rangers offer many programs to visitors, as follows:

- **Discovering Rocky:** This one is made for those who wish to become a junior ranger. A ranger will guide you to learn everything to know about the Rocky Mountains. It's available every day and lasts for around 30 minutes.

- **Bird Walks:** This program is available for people who would like to learn about the birds that reside in the park. It's open only on Wednesdays and Fridays, which lasts for an hour. You need to go to Upper Beaver Meadows to join this program.

- **Lily Lake Stroll:** A ranger will take you on a walk along Lily Lake, where you may learn about its history and nature. It's available on Tuesdays and Thursdays. Additionally, it takes about an hour to complete.

- **Family Discovery Hike:** This family-friendly program is made for those who want to go hiking guided by a ranger. It starts at Moraine Park Discovery Center and is available every day. It doesn't take too long either since it lasts around 40 minutes.

- **Bighorn Basics:** The park is home to a large bighorn population. This program shares how they can adapt and survive even with the changing weather conditions. It can be accessed every day and is only 20 minutes long.

- **Fire to Flowers:** Available from Saturday to Monday, this ranger program tells you the history of Beaver Meadows, from how the weather influences its development to how the flowers flourish in the area. Additionally, it takes an hour to finish.

- **Birding for All:** This is another program for bird enthusiasts. Available on Thursday each week, you'll go birdwatching accompanied by a park ranger. You have to go to Lily Lake to join this activity.

- **Explore Sprague Lake:** This lake is a famous attraction in the park where you can do water activities and even hike on a designated trail surrounding it. In this program, you'll walk along the lake with a ranger who will share about its history and features. It's available from Monday to Sunday, and it lasts for less than an hour.

Furthermore, there are also some programs on the west side. All of these programs are available from Monday to Sunday, but they begin at different hours. What are they?

- **West Side Stories:** A ranger will take you around the western part of the park and share its history and culture. Starting at 4 p.m., this program is only around 30 minutes.

- **Critter Chat:** You'll walk around the Kawuneeche Valley to see the various wildlife that reside there. It begins at 1:30 p.m. and lasts under 30 minutes.

- **Glimpse into the Kawuneeche Valley:** Walking along the Kawuneeche Valley, you'll find out more about its history. Starting at 3 p.m., this talk is only 20 minutes long.

- **Life on the Homestead:** This is a program about the Holzwarth family and how they built their homestead (*Ranger-led programs*, 2023). It starts at 11 a.m. and ends in under 15 minutes.

Not only on the east and west sides, but there are also a couple of programs that start at the Alpine Visitor Center, as follows:

- **Wild Mountain Weather:** In this program, a ranger will teach you about the park's weather conditions and how to prepare yourself for various activities. It's available on Tuesdays, Wednesdays, Thursdays, and Saturdays.

- **Tundra Nature Walk:** A ranger will lead you to a tundra area and share everything to know about it. You may join Sunday to Friday.

Horseback Riding

If you want an anti-mainstream way to explore the park, horseback riding is a great way for that. However, if you're not experienced with horses yet, you don't need to worry because the park offers some guided tours for visitors. Opening in late May or early June, the park is home to Glacier Creek Stables and Moraine Park Stables, where you may reserve a horse tour.

However, before you reserve a tour, you must consider where you want to go and what destinations you wish to visit first. Since the stables begin from different points, they'll give you distinct experiences. You'll also visit different places depending on the stable you choose. This means that you must research everything before your trip so that you can decide the one suitable for your needs and schedules.

Fishing

Since the park's development, fishing has grown in popularity among visitors. This is because the park is filled with various lakes, rivers, and streams. There are many fish species that inhabit its waters, but the most popular ones for fishing are cutthroat trout, brook trout, and rainbow trout (*Rocky Mountain fishing*, 2022).

If you're over 16 years old, you must obtain a fishing license from the State of Colorado. However, you need to pay a fee to get it, starting at $10 per person. These prices will depend on your age and how long the license lasts. Moreover, there are also some fishing regulations based on where you fish, and you must check them online beforehand.

If you're unsure where to fish at the park, here are some recommendations:

- **Big Thompson River:** This river is very long, so you can find solitude if you want privacy. The most common fish here is rainbow and brown trout (Durrant, 2022). It's also great for those who like adventure since the river stretches to the backcountry area.

- **Sprague Lake:** All types of trout are available in this lake, which makes it a popular destination for fishing. It's also famous for its stunning views, and many visitors even choose the area for hiking.

- **Ouzel Creek:** If you like to fish in a smaller body of water, this stream can be a great option. However, you have to hike to this creek, so it's not very easy to reach. This creek has a big population of brookies (Durrant, 2022).

- **Thunder Lake:** Situated in a remote area, this lake is popular among backpackers. Most visitors who fish here need to pass through challenging terrains. However, it can be rewarding because the lake offers beautiful views of various mountain peaks.

Key Takeaways

- Rocky Mountain National Park was developed and established in 1915 in the State of Colorado.

- The human history within the park started over 11,000 years ago.

- The park has a vast land that covers over 400 square miles.

- The most famous attractions there are Trail Ridge Road, Estes Park, and Bear Lake.

- Before your vacation, you must know some basic information first, from its opening seasons and hours to its accommodations and campgrounds.

- There are various things to do at the park, including hiking, driving, watching wildlife, picnicking, joining a ranger program, horseback riding, and fishing.

Now that we've arrived at the last chapter, it's time to jump to the conclusion!

Conclusion

Congratulations on arriving at the conclusion of the book. I hope that you had fun and learned some essential information about the popular West Coast national parks. A vacation doesn't need to be expensive because the entrance fees of these parks are budget-friendly. As you have come to the end of the book, have you decided on which national park to visit first? It's time to get ready, pack up the essentials, and get away from your busy life!

Let's go over some of the key ideas that I've talked about in this book. I've explained that there are six popular national parks on the West Coast, including Yellowstone, Grand Teton, Yosemite, Grand Canyon, Mount Rainier, and Rocky Mountain. Each one has its own characteristics and traits, from being filled with mountainous areas to having lakes, rivers, and ponds. Based on your preference, you should visit the ones that meet your needs—or make plans to visit all of them!

Before your vacation, you have to organize your trip first. I've explained the essential information in this book so your trip can go smoothly. From the national parks' operating seasons and hours to their campgrounds. Not only that, but you've figured out what types of activities to do in each park. Every park has certain activities available to visitors from summer to winter. However, not all parks have winter activities, so keep that in mind.

If you enjoy water activities, you can go for a swim in the lakes, fish in the streams, or boat in the rivers. If you wish to sweat more and do something more active, you can hike, bike, or join a ranger program. During the winter months, you may opt for other activities like skiing, snowboarding, or even sledding at one of these parks. Whatever you decide to do, every one of these activities can be accessed.

Furthermore, it will be worthwhile to visit as many national parks as you can because each one has distinctive features and a different history. They can be wonderful destinations for day trips or even overnight stays. And you don't need to worry about getting bored because there are various things to do wherever you decide to go. Are you prepared to relax and get into your next vacation?

If you discover useful information and guidance in this book, please leave me a review!

Glossary

Backcountry: An area where there are few human activities or somewhere that is not developed yet.

Canyon: A small and deep valley with cliff-like walls.

Critter: It refers to an animal.

Cross-country: Moving from a country's area to a different side.

Dome: A formation shaped with a circular design.

Fossil: A trace of prehistoric or ancient existence preserved by nature.

Geyser: A hot spring shooting boiling water from the ground.

Glacier: Large and steadily flowing masses of ice.

Homestead: It is a land with a house and farm.

Ranger: Someone who works to maintain and preserve national parks.

RV: A recreational vehicle that is equipped with a living space.

Trailhead: A trail's starting point.

Tundra: A cold land where no trees can grow.

References

About Grand Canyon animals. (n.d.). Explore the Canyon. https://explorethecanyon.com/grand-canyon-wildlife-vegetation/

Absolon, M. (2020, November 30). *Grand Canyon bicycle*. My Grand Canyon Park. https://www.mygrandcanyonpark.com/things-to-do/biking/by-bicycle/

Adams Falls Trail. (2023). All Trails. https://www.alltrails.com/trail/us/colorado/adams-falls-trail?u=m

Alberta Falls Trail. (2023). All Trails. https://www.alltrails.com/trail/us/colorado/alberta-falls-trail?u=m

Anderson, M. (2023, August 11). Grand Canyon National Park. Britannica. https://www.britannica.com/place/Grand-Canyon-National-Park

Animals. (2017, January 19). National Park Service. https://www.nps.gov/yose/learn/nature/animals.htm

Aspen Ridge – Boulder Ridge. (2023, August 2). National Park Service. https://www.nps.gov/thingstodo/aspen-boulderridge.htm

Bear Lake Road scenic drive in Rocky Mountain National Park. (n.d.). Rocky Mountain National Park. https://www.rockymountainnationalpark.com/gallery/drive-bear/

Best places for birding in Yosemite Mariposa County. (2020, May 12). Yosemite Mariposa County. https://www.yosemite.com/best-locations-for-birding-in-yosemite-mariposa-county/

Best places for fishing in Yosemite. (n.d.). Scenic Wonders. https://www.scenicwonders.com/yosemite-park-attractions/yosemite-fishing

Best skiing trails in Mount Rainier National Park. (2023). All Trails. https://www.alltrails.com/parks/us/washington/mount-rainier-national-park/skiing

Bicycling at Mount Rainier. (2022, April 8). National Park Service. https://www.nps.gov/mora/planyourvisit/bicycling.htm

Bicycling safety and regulations. (2022, June 27). National Park Service. https://www.nps.gov/mora/planyourvisit/bicycling-safety-regulations.htm

Bierstadt Lake. (2022, July 13). National Park Service. https://www.nps.gov/thingstodo/romo_bierstadtlake.htm

Biking in the park. (2023, March 15). National Park Service. https://www.nps.gov/grte/planyourvisit/bike.htm

Biking. (2023, June 14). National Park Service. https://www.nps.gov/yell/planyourvisit/bicycling.htm

Birdwatching. (2023, February 28). National Park Service. https://www.nps.gov/yose/planyourvisit/birdwatching.htm

Black to the park. (2023). The Bronze Chapter. https://thebronzechapter.org/black-to-the-park/

Bliss, A. (2023, July 11). *Where to stay in Estes Park (best places and areas in 2023).* Travel Lemming. https://travellemming.com/where-to-stay-in-estes-park/

Boat on a lake. (2023, July 12). National Park Service. https://www.nps.gov/yell/planyourvisit/boating.htm

Bridalveil Fall Trail. (2021, September 28). National Park Service. https://www.nps.gov/yose/planyourvisit/bridalveilfalltrail.htm

Brief park history. (2015, December 1). National Park Service. https://www.nps.gov/romo/learn/historyculture/brief.htm

Bright Angel Lodge and Cabins. (2020, April 28). My Grand Canyon Park. https://www.mygrandcanyonpark.com/where-to-stay-camp-eat/hotels-cabins/inside-the-park/bright-angel-lodge-cabins/

Campgrounds. (2023, August 4). National Park Service. https://www.nps.gov/yose/planyourvisit/campgrounds.htm

Camping in Grand Canyon National Park. (2023, July 24). National Park Service. https://www.nps.gov/grca/planyourvisit/camping.htm

Camping. (2022, December 27). National Park Service. https://www.nps.gov/grte/planyourvisit/camping.htm

Camping. (2023, June 30). National Park Service. https://www.nps.gov/yell/planyourvisit/campgrounds.htm

Canyon Motel and RV Park. (2023). The Canyon Motel. https://thecanyonmotel.com/

Catch a fish. (2023, June 14). National Park Service. https://www.nps.gov/yell/planyourvisit/fishing.htm

Chasm Falls via Old Fall River Road. (2023). All Trails. https://www.alltrails.com/trail/us/colorado/chasm-falls-trail-via-old-fall-river-road?u=m

Climbing and mountaineering. (2019, October 23). National Park Service. https://www.nps.gov/grte/planyourvisit/climb.htm

Complete a Mount Rainier junior ranger booklet. (2022, November 8). National Park Service. https://www.nps.gov/thingstodo/complete-a-mount-rainier-junior-ranger-booklet.htm

Cook's Meadow Loop. (2022, May 17). National Park Service. https://www.nps.gov/yose/planyourvisit/cooksmeadowtrail.htm

Croft, A. (2022, June 28). *Animals in Yellowstone National Park: The complete guide.* A-Z Animals. https://a-z-animals.com/blog/animals-in-yellowstone-national-park/

Cross-country skiing. (2023). Travel Yosemite. https://www.travelyosemite.com/winter/badger-pass-ski-area/cross-country-skiing/

Cub Lake Loop Trail. (2023). All Trails. https://www.alltrails.com/trail/us/colorado/cub-lake-trail-loop?u=m

Cultural history. (2019, October 23). National Park Service. https://www.nps.gov/grte/learn/historyculture/cultural.htm

Curry Village ice skating rink. (2023). Travel Yosemite. https://www.travelyosemite.com/winter/curry-village-ice-skating-rink/

Curry Village. (2023). Travel Yosemite. https://www.travelyosemite.com/lodging/curry-village/

Day hikes in the Canyon area. (2020, October 5). National Park Service. https://www.nps.gov/tripideas/day-hikes-in-the-canyon-area.htm

Day hikes in the Grant and West Thumb area. (2020, October 6). National Park Service. https://www.nps.gov/tripideas/day-hikes-in-the-grant-area.htm

Day hikes in the Lake and Fishing Bridge area. (2020, October 6). National Park Service. https://www.nps.gov/tripideas/day-hikes-in-the-lake-area.htm

Day hikes in the Madison area. (2018, June 28). National Park Service. https://www.nps.gov/tripideas/day-hikes-in-the-madison-area.htm

Day hikes in the Mammoth area. (2021, June 2). National Park Service. https://www.nps.gov/tripideas/day-hikes-in-the-mammoth-area.htm

Day hikes in the Old Faithful area. (2020, October 6). National Park Service. https://www.nps.gov/tripideas/day-hikes-in-the-old-faithful-area.htm

Day hikes in the Tower and Northeast area. (2023, May 1). National Park Service. https://www.nps.gov/tripideas/day-hikes-in-the-tower-area.htm

Day hiking at Mount Rainier. (2023, May 4). National Park Service. https://www.nps.gov/mora/planyourvisit/day-hiking-at-mount-rainier.htm

Day, A. (2023, June 9). *Summer in Washington's parks: Best national parks picnic sites.* Washington's National Park Fund. https://wnpf.org/2023/06/09/summer-in-washingtons-parks-best-national-park-picnic-sites/

Devil's Gulch scenic drive. (2023). Rocky Mountain National Park. https://www.rockymountainnationalpark.com/gallery/drive-devils/

Dietrickx, K. (2015, November 4). *59 facts about our national parks.* Outdoor Project. https://www.outdoorproject.com/articles/59-fun-facts-about-our-national-parks

Discover wildflowers. (2023, August 18). National Park Service. https://www.nps.gov/mora/planyourvisit/wildflower-status.htm

Downhill skiing and snowboarding. (2023). Travel Yosemite. https://www.travelyosemite.com/winter/badger-pass-ski-area/downhill-skiing-snowboarding/

Durrant, S. (2022). *7 best places to fly fish in Rocky Mountain National Park.* Guide Recommended. https://guiderecommended.com/fly-fish-rocky-mountain-national-park/

Durrant, S. (2023). *7 best places to fly fish in Grand Teton National Park.* Guide Recommended. https://guiderecommended.com/fly-fish-grand-teton-national-park/

Eating and sleeping. (2016, June 10). National Park Service. https://www.nps.gov/romo/planyourvisit/eatingsleeping.htm

Ecology of Rocky Mountain National Park. (n.d.). US Geological Survey. https://www.usgs.gov/geology-and-ecology-of-national-parks/ecology-rocky-mountain-national-park#:~:text=Rocky%20Mountain%20hosts%20more%20than,adapted%20to%20various%20mountain%20ecosystems.

El Tovar Hotel in Grand Canyon National Park. (2018, April 4). My Grand Canyon Park. https://www.mygrandcanyonpark.com/where-to-stay-camp-eat/hotels-cabins/inside-the-park/el-tovar-hotel/

Entrance passes. (2023, July 24). National Park Service. https://www.nps.gov/planyourvisit/passes.htm

Escape to the mountains. (n.d.). The Maxwell Inn. https://themaxwellinn.com/accommodations/

Experience the best of the Grand Canyon. (n.d.). Grand Canyon Squire. https://www.grandcanyonsquire.com/

Explore on two wheels. (2023). Travel Yosemite. https://www.travelyosemite.com/things-to-do/biking/

Explore thermal basins. (2021, May 3). National Park Service. https://www.nps.gov/yell/planyourvisit/thermal-basin-exploring.htm

Fees & passes. (2023, June 22). National Park Service. https://www.nps.gov/grte/planyourvisit/fees.htm

Fink, M. (2022, April 19). *Explore the beautiful wildlife of Grand Teton National Park.* https://jacksonholewildlifesafaris.com/grand-teton-national-park-wildlife/

Fiorentino, F. (2023, February 20). *10 top attractions in Yosemite National Park.* Touropia. https://www.touropia.com/yosemite-attractions/

Fishing. (n.d.). Visit Rainier. https://visitrainier.com/activities/summer-activities/fishing/

Fishing. (2022, August 4). National Park Service. https://www.nps.gov/grte/planyourvisit/fish.htm

Fishing. (2023, February 21). National Park Service. https://www.nps.gov/yose/planyourvisit/fishing.htm

Fishing and boating. (2021, April 8). National Park Service. https://www.nps.gov/mora/planyourvisit/fishing-and-boating.htm

Forks of Cascade Canyon. (2022, May 16). National Park Service. https://www.nps.gov/thingstodo/cascadecanyon.htm

Get on the water. (2023, April 3). National Park Service. https://www.nps.gov/grte/planyourvisit/boat.htm

Glacier Point Ski Hut. (2023). Travel Yosemite. https://www.travelyosemite.com/lodging/glacier-point-ski-hut/

Grand Canyon fees and passes. (2023, June 7). National Park Service. https://www.nps.gov/grca/planyourvisit/fees.htm

Grand Canyon guided Jeep tours. (n.d.). Grand Canyon Guru. https://grandcanyonguru.com/grand-canyon-jeep-tours

Grand Canyon history. (2023). Grand Canyon Guru. https://grandcanyonguru.com/learning/grand-canyon-history

Grand Canyon of the Yellowstone. (n.d.). US News. https://travel.usnews.com/Yellowstone_National_Park_WY/Things_To_Do/Grand_Canyon_of_the_Yellowstone_11281/

Grand Canyon opening hours and seasons. (n.d.). The Canyon. https://www.thecanyon.com/operating-hours

Grand Canyon operating hours and season. (2023, July 24). National Park Service. https://www.nps.gov/grca/planyourvisit/hours.htm

Grand Canyon permits and reservations. (2023, July 25). National Park Service. https://www.nps.gov/grca/planyourvisit/permitsandreservations.htm

Grand Canyon railway. (2023). Flagstaff. https://www.flagstaff.com/grand-canyon-railway#:~:text=every%20American%20should%20see.%E2%80%9D%20The,and%20we%20recommend%20bringing%20layers

Grand Canyon river rafting experience. (n.d.). River and Adventures. https://www.riveradventures.com/grand-canyon-rafting/grand-canyon-river-rafting-experience/

Grand Canyon western adventure. (2023). Grand Canyon Western Ranch. https://grandcanyonwesternranch.com/

Grand Teton National Park operating hours and seasons. (n.d.). National Park Guru. https://www.nationalparkguru.com/national-parks/grand-teton-national-park/grand-teton-national-park-information/grand-teton-national-park-operating-hours-seasons/

Grand Teton operating hours and seasons. (2023, August 2). National Park Service. https://www.nps.gov/grte/planyourvisit/hours.htm

Grand Teton permits and reservations. (2023, August 14). National Park Service. https://www.nps.gov/grte/planyourvisit/permitsandreservations.htm

Guided bus tours. (2023). Travel Yosemite. https://www.travelyosemite.com/things-to-do/guided-bus-tours/

Half Dome day hike. (2023, April 14). National Park Service. https://www.nps.gov/yose/planyourvisit/halfdome.htm

Half Dome permits for day hikers. (2023, June 15). National Park Service. https://www.nps.gov/yose/planyourvisit/hdpermits.htm

Hein, A. (2014, November 8). *The establishment of Grand Teton National Park.* WyoHistory. https://www.wyohistory.org/encyclopedia/establishment-grand-teton-national-park

Hermitage Point. (2022, May 18). National Park Service. https://www.nps.gov/thingstodo/hermitagepoint.htm

High Sierra Camps. (2023). Travel Yosemite. https://www.travelyosemite.com/lodging/high-sierra-camps/

Highway 7 scenic drive in Rocky Mountain National Park. (n.d.). Rocky Mountain National Park. https://www.rockymountainnationalpark.com/gallery/drive-hwy7/

Hike Deer Mountain. (2022, July 15). National Park Service. https://www.nps.gov/thingstodo/romo_deermountain.htm

Hike Fern Lake. (2022, July 13). National Park Service. https://www.nps.gov/thingstodo/romo_fernlake.htm

Hike the East Shore Trail. (2022, July 15). National Park Service. https://www.nps.gov/thingstodo/romo_eastshoretrail.htm

Hike to Bear Lake. (2022, July 13). National Park Service. https://www.nps.gov/thingstodo/romo_bearlake.htm

Hike to Cascade Falls. (2023, July 15). National Park Service. https://www.nps.gov/thingstodo/romo_cascadefalls.htm

Hike to Chasm Lake. (2022, July 15). National Park Service. https://www.nps.gov/thingstodo/romo_chasmlake.htm

Hike to Dream Lake. (2023, August 17). National Park Service. https://www.nps.gov/thingstodo/romo_dreamlake.htm

Hike to Estes Cone. (2022, July 20). National Park Service. https://www.nps.gov/thingstodo/romo_estescone.htm

Hike to Flattop Mountain. (2022, July 20). National Park Service. https://www.nps.gov/thingstodo/romo_flattopmountain.htm

Hike to Gem Lake. (2023, August 17). National Park Service. https://www.nps.gov/thingstodo/romo_gemlake.htm

Hike to Granite Falls. (2022, July 20). National Park Service. https://www.nps.gov/thingstodo/romo_granitefalls.htm

Hike to Lake Haiyaha. (2023, August 17). National Park Service. https://www.nps.gov/thingstodo/romo_lakehaiyaha.htm

Hike to Mills Lake. (2023, August 21). National Park Service. https://www.nps.gov/thingstodo/romo_millslake.htm

Hike to Odessa Lake. (2022, July 20). National Park Service. https://www.nps.gov/thingstodo/romo_odessa.htm

Hike to the Loch. (2022, July 20). National Park Service. https://www.nps.gov/thingstodo/romo_theloch.htm

Hike to the Pool. (2022, July 21). National Park Service. https://www.nps.gov/thingstodo/romo_thepool.htm

Hike to the Twin Sisters Summit. (2022, July 15). National Park Service. https://www.nps.gov/thingstodo/romo_twinsisters.htm

Hike to Ypsilon Lake. (2022, July 21). National Park Service. https://www.nps.gov/thingstodo/romo_ypsilonlake.htm

Hiking. (2023, August 2). National Park Service. https://www.nps.gov/grte/planyourvisit/hike.htm

History & culture. (2021, March 15). National Park Service. https://www.nps.gov/yell/learn/historyculture/index.htm

History of Rocky Mountain National Park. (2023). Go Grand Lake. https://gograndlake.com/history-of-rocky-mountain-national-park/

Holden, C. (2021, August 10). *Entrance fees and where to get your park pass for Yellowstone.* Yellowstone Park. https://www.yellowstonepark.com/park/faqs/fees/

Horseback and mule riding. (2023). Travel Yosemite. https://www.travelyosemite.com/things-to-do/horseback-mule-

riding/#:~:text=Beyond%20hiking%2C%20the%20best%20w
ay,be%20in%20good%20physical%20condition.

Horseback rides in Rocky Mountain National Park. (n.d.). Rocky Mountain National Park. https://www.rockymountainnationalpark.com/gallery/guide-horse/

Housekeeping Camp. (2023). Travel Yosemite. https://www.travelyosemite.com/lodging/housekeeping-camp/

Hualapai Lodge at Peach Springs. (2017, April 11). My Grand Canyon Park. https://www.mygrandcanyonpark.com/where-to-stay-camp-eat/hotels-cabins/grand-canyon-west/hualapai-lodge/

Hualapai Ranch at Peach Springs, Arizona. (2017, April 11). My Grand Canyon Park. https://www.mygrandcanyonpark.com/where-to-stay-camp-eat/hotels-cabins/grand-canyon-west/hualapai-ranch/

Human history of Rocky Mountain National Park. (n.d.). Rocky Mountain National Park. https://www.rockymountainnationalpark.com/gallery/human-history/

John. (2021, February 6). *The complete Grand Teton wildlife viewing guide.* Park Ranger John. https://www.parkrangerjohn.com/the-complete-grand-teton-wildlife-viewing-guide/

Jones, J. (2023a, July 27). *12 best campgrounds in Yellowstone National Park.* Well Planned Journey. https://www.wellplannedjourney.com/best-campgrounds-in-yellowstone/

Jones, J. (2023b, July 27). *Where to stay when visiting Grand Teton National Park in 2023.* Well Planned Journey.

https://www.wellplannedjourney.com/where-to-stay-in-grand-teton/

Jones, J. (2023c, July 27). *25 best things to do in Grand Teton National Park.* https://www.wellplannedjourney.com/things-to-do-in-grand-teton/

Jones, J. (2023d, January 16). *18 best hikes in Grand Teton National Park.* Well Planned Journey. https://www.wellplannedjourney.com/best-hikes-in-grand-teton/

Julie. (2022, November 4). *14 amazing things to do in Mount Rainier National Park.* Earth Trekkers. https://www.earthtrekkers.com/best-things-to-do-in-mount-rainier-national-park/

Julie. (2023a, July 12). *11 epic things to do on the South Rim of the Grand Canyon.* Earth Trekkers. https://www.earthtrekkers.com/best-things-to-do-in-the-grand-canyon-south-rim/

Julie. (2023b, July 8). *15 best things to do in Grand Teton National Park.* Earth Trekkers. https://www.earthtrekkers.com/best-things-to-do-grand-teton-national-park/

Julie. (2023c, July 21). *15 best day hikes in Grand Teton National Park.* Earth Trekkers. https://www.earthtrekkers.com/best-day-hikes-grand-teton/

Kachina Lodge. (2015, November 19). My Grand Canyon Park. https://www.mygrandcanyonpark.com/where-to-stay-camp-eat/hotels-cabins/inside-the-park/kachina-lodge/

Kwak-Hefferan, E. (2021, February 3). *10 best things to do in the Grand Canyon.* My Grand Canyon Park. https://www.mygrandcanyonpark.com/things-to-do/park-itineraries/top-ten/?scope=anon

Liz, N. (2020, September 10). *In depth guide: Car-free biking in Jackson Hole and Grand Teton National Park*. Roaming the Americas. https://roamingtheamericas.com/bike-paths-jackson-hole-grand-teton-national-park/

Lodging, cabins, and camping. (2023). Mt Rainier. https://mt-rainier.com/lodging/

Lodging. (2022, December 27). National Park Service. https://www.nps.gov/grte/planyourvisit/lodging.htm

Lodging. (2023). Visit Grand County. https://www.visitgrandcounty.com/trips/eat-and-stay/lodging

Madaj, A. (2022, January 20). *Tips for safe hiking in Yellowstone*. The Travel. https://www.thetravel.com/tips-for-hiking-safely-in-yellowstone/#hike-in-groups

Marion Lake. (2023, August 2). National Park Service. https://www.nps.gov/thingstodo/marionlake.htm

Maswik Lodge. (2022, March 13). My Grand Canyon Park. https://www.mygrandcanyonpark.com/where-to-stay-camp-eat/hotels-cabins/inside-the-park/maswik-lodge/

Maxwell, A. (2020, June 26). *Guide: Yellowstone National Park camping tips*. Current Camper. https://currentcamper.com/10-tips-for-yellowstone-national-park-camping/

Meander down the Merced River. (2023). Travel Yosemite. https://www.travelyosemite.com/things-to-do/rafting/

Megan. (2023, May 21). *9 best hikes in Yosemite National Park*. Rei. https://destinations.rei.com/local-tips/best-hikes-in-yosemite-national-park

Mirror Lake Trail. (2022, May 17). National Park Service. https://www.nps.gov/yose/planyourvisit/mirrorlaketrail.htm

Mishev, D. (2023, June 14). *Where to stay in Yellowstone.* Yellowstone National Park Lodges. https://www.yellowstonenationalparklodges.com/connect/yellowstone-hot-spot/where-to-stay/

Mount Rainier animals. (2021, January 11). National Park Service. https://www.nps.gov/mora/learn/nature/animals.htm

Mount Rainier campgrounds. (2023, August 21). National Park Service. https://www.nps.gov/mora/planyourvisit/campgrounds.htm

Mount Rainier climbing. (2023, June 5). National Park Service. https://www.nps.gov/mora/planyourvisit/climbing.htm

Mount Rainier ecology. (2023). US Geological Survey. https://www.usgs.gov/geology-and-ecology-of-national-parks/mount-rainier-ecology#:~:text=big%2Deared%20bat.-,NPS.,the%20Park%20in%20100%20years

Mount Rainier fees and passes. (2023, July 11). National Park Service. https://www.nps.gov/mora/planyourvisit/fees.htm

Mount Rainier history. (2023, August 3). National Park Service. https://www.nps.gov/mora/learn/historyculture/mount-rainier-history.htm#:~:text=Captain%20George%20Vancouver%20of%20the,friend%2C%20Rear%20Admiral%20Peter%20Rainier.

Mount Rainier lodging. (2023, July 25). National Park Service. https://www.nps.gov/mora/planyourvisit/lodging.htm

Mount Rainier operating hours and seasons. (2023, August 21). National Park Service. https://www.nps.gov/mora/planyourvisit/hours.htm

Mount Rainier permits and reservations. (2023, June 7). National Park Service. https://www.nps.gov/mora/planyourvisit/permitsandreservations.htm

Mount Rainier picnic areas. (2023, July 13). National Park Service. https://www.nps.gov/mora/planyourvisit/picnic-areas.htm

Mount Rainier Wildflowers. (n.d.). Visit Rainier. https://visitrainier.com/activities/wildflowers-and-wildlife/wildflowers/

Mount Rainier wildlife safety. (2023, January 23). National Park Service. https://www.nps.gov/mora/planyourvisit/wildlife.htm

Mountain biking. (n.d.). Visit Rainier. https://visitrainier.com/activities/summer-activities/biking/mountain-biking/

Mule trips. (2021, February 2021). National Park Service. https://www.nps.gov/grca/planyourvisit/mule_trips.htm

Natural features & ecosystems. (2018, May 7). National Park Service. https://www.nps.gov/romo/learn/nature/naturalfeaturesandecosystems.htm

Norberg, D. (2020, October 13). *Mount Rainier National Park.* History Link. https://www.historylink.org/file/21111

Onion, A., Sullivan, M., Mullen, M., & Zapata, C. (2019, July 29). *Grand Teton National Park is established.* History. https://www.history.com/this-day-in-history/grand-teton-national-park-is-established

Onion, A., Sullivan, M., Mullen, M., & Zapata, C. (2020, September 29). *Grand Canyon.* History. https://www.history.com/topics/landmarks/grand-canyon

Operating hours & seasons. (2023, August 1). National Park Service. https://www.nps.gov/yell/planyourvisit/hours.htm

Paintbrush Canyon – Cascade Canyon Loop. (2022, May 17). National Park
Service.
https://www.nps.gov/thingstodo/paintbrushcascade.htm

Park campgrounds. (2023). Jackson Hole WY.
https://www.jacksonholewy.net/park_campgrounds/

Park statistics. (2023, June 22). National Park Service.
https://www.nps.gov/grca/learn/management/statistics.htm

Parker, C. (2023a, July 27). *20 epic things to do in the Grand Canyon*. US
News.
https://travel.usnews.com/Grand_Canyon_AZ/Things_To_D
o/

Parker, C. (2023b, June 29). *17 epic things to do in Yellowstone National
Park*. US News.
https://travel.usnews.com/Yellowstone_National_Park_WY/
Things_To_Do/

Peglar, T. (2021a, January 15). *How Yosemite came to be*. My Yosemite
Park. https://www.myyosemitepark.com/park/history/how-
yosemite-became/

Peglar, T. (2021b, October 24). *Lake Yellowstone hotel and cabins in
Yellowstone*. Yellowstone Park.
https://www.yellowstonepark.com/where-to-stay-camp-
eat/hotels-cabins/inside-yellowstone-park/yellowstone-lake-
hotel/

Peglar, T. (2022a, January 20). *Fun on the water of Grand Teton National
Park*. Yellowstone Park.
https://www.yellowstonepark.com/things-to-do/rafting-water-
activities/grand-teton-water-activities/

Peglar, T. (2022b, April 22). *8 best historic hotels in and near Yellowstone*.
Yellowstone Park. https://www.yellowstonepark.com/where-

to-stay-camp-eat/hotels-cabins/inside-yellowstone-park/see-a-historic-hotel/?scope=anon

Peglar, T. (2022c, March 2). *Canyon lodge and cabins inside Yellowstone.* Yellowstone Park. https://www.yellowstonepark.com/where-to-stay-camp-eat/hotels-cabins/inside-yellowstone-park/canyon-lodge-cabins/

Peglar, T. (2023a, April 28). *Which entrance should I take into Rocky Mountain National Park?* My Colorado Parks. https://www.mycoloradoparks.com/park/faqs/rmnp-entrances/

Peglar, T. (2023b, January 2023). *15 campgrounds – ultimate Grand Canyon camping guide.* My Grand Canyon Park. https://www.mygrandcanyonpark.com/where-to-stay-camp-eat/camping-rv/grand-canyon-camping-guide/

Peglar, T. (2023c, March 15). *Phantom Ranch at the bottom of Grand Canyon.* My Grand Canyon Park. https://www.mygrandcanyonpark.com/where-to-stay-camp-eat/hotels-cabins/inside-the-park/phantom-ranch-grand-canyon/?scope=anon

Perkiss, D. (n.d.). *Top 8 reasons to visit national parks.* Great Value Vacations. https://www.greatvaluevacations.com/travel-inspiration/top-reasons-to-visit-national-parks

Permits & reservations. (2023, march 1). National Park Service. https://www.nps.gov/grte/planyourvisit/permitsandreservations.htm

Pietrzak, K. (2023, July 8). *11 best places to see wildlife in Rocky Mountain National Park.* Volumes and Voyages. https://volumesandvoyages.com/best-places-to-see-wildlife-in-rocky-mountain-national-park/

Places to get interagency passes. (n.d.). National Park Service. https://www.nps.gov/planyourvisit/pickup-pass-locations.htm?&p=1&v=0

Pletcher, K. (2023, February 28). *Mount Rainier National Park.* Britannica. https://www.britannica.com/place/Mount-Rainier-National-Park

Povey, K. (2022, July 11). *Top ten spots for wildlife viewing in Washington's national parks this summer.* Washington's National Park Fund. https://wnpf.org/2022/07/11/top-ten-spots-for-wildlife-viewing-in-washingtons-national-parks-this-summer/

Provozin, E. (2022a, April 11). *Birdwatching in Yosemite.* Rove. https://rove.me/to/yosemite/birdwatching

Provozin, E. (2022b, April 8). *Fishing in Yosemite.* Rove. https://rove.me/to/yosemite/fishing

Puliti, L. (2022, February 22). *Where to stay at the Grand Canyon? Tips for choosing a hotel.* Travel in USA. https://www.travelinusa.us/grand-canyon-where-to-stay/#Hotels_in_the_South_Rim

Rampart Ridge Loop Trail. (2023). All Trails. https://www.alltrails.com/trail/us/washington/rampart-ridge-loop-trail?u=m

Rams Horn Village Resort. (n.d.). Luxury Estes Park Cabins. https://www.luxuryestesparkcabins.com/

Ranger-led programs. (2023, August 7). National Park Service. https://www.nps.gov/romo/planyourvisit/ranger-led-programs.htm

Rashmi. (2023). *10 of the best attractions in the Grand Canyon.* Wildlife Zones. https://wildlifezones.com/best-attractions-in-the-grand-canyon/

Ride a bike in Yosemite National Park. (2021, November 2). My Yosemite Park. https://www.myyosemitepark.com/things-to-do/summer-activities/go-bicycling-in-yosemite-park/

Ride a horse. (2023, May 1). National Park Service. https://www.nps.gov/yell/planyourvisit/horseride.htm

Ride a snowmobile or snowcoach. (2023, January 24). National Park Service. https://www.nps.gov/yell/planyourvisit/snowmobiles-snowcoaches.htm

Rock climbing. (2023, June 29). National Park Service. https://www.nps.gov/yose/planyourvisit/climbing.htm

Rocky Mountain campgrounds. (2023, August 17). National Park Service. https://www.nps.gov/romo/planyourvisit/camping.htm

Rocky Mountain fees and passes. (2023, July 7). National Park Service. https://www.nps.gov/romo/planyourvisit/fees.htm

Rocky Mountain fishing. (2022, May 27). National Park Service. https://www.nps.gov/romo/planyourvisit/fishing.htm

Rocky Mountain operating hours and seasons. (2022, December 21). National Park Service. https://www.nps.gov/romo/planyourvisit/hours.htm

Rocky Mountain. (2023, May 26). National Park Service. https://www.nps.gov/romo/planyourvisit/permitsandreservations.htm

Rocky Mountain picnicking. (2023, July 13). National Park Service. https://www.nps.gov/romo/planyourvisit/picnicking.htm

Rocky Mountain visitor centers. (2023, May 23). National Park Service. https://www.nps.gov/romo/planyourvisit/visitorcenters.htm

Rocky Mountain wildlife viewing. (2023, April 7). National Park Service. https://www.nps.gov/romo/planyourvisit/wildlife_view.htm

Ruland, M. (2022, September 16). *A grander stay at Yavapai Lodge.* My Grand Canyon Park. https://www.mygrandcanyonpark.com/where-to-stay-camp-eat/hotels-cabins/inside-the-park/yavapai-lodge/

Scenic drives. (2021, December 17). National Park Service. https://www.nps.gov/romo/planyourvisit/scenic-drives.htm

Singh, L. (2023). *Yosemite's 13 must-see attractions.* Travel Channel. https://www.travelchannel.com/destinations/us/ca/photos/yosemite-attractions

6 best things to do in Mount Rainier National Park. (2021, February 11). US News. https://travel.usnews.com/Mount_Rainier_National_Park_WA/Things_To_Do/

16 best things to do in Rocky Mountain National Park. (2023, February 21). US News. https://travel.usnews.com/Rocky_Mountain_National_Park_CO/Things_To_Do/

Ski and snowshoe. (2021, February 18). National Park Service. https://www.nps.gov/yell/planyourvisit/skiing-and-snowshoeing.htm

Sledding and snow tubing in Yosemite Country. (2020, April 30). My Yosemite Park. https://www.myyosemitepark.com/things-to-do/winter-activities/sledding-and-snow-tubing/

Snell, M. (2022, May 26). *10 amazing things to do in Yellowstone National Park during the summer.* Travel Awaits. https://www.travelawaits.com/2766806/things-to-do-yellowstone-national-park-during-summer/

Snow Creek Trail. (2022, May 19). National Park Service. https://www.nps.gov/yose/planyourvisit/snowcreektrail.htm

Snow tubing. (2023). Travel Yosemite. https://www.travelyosemite.com/winter/badger-pass-ski-area/snow-tubing/

South Rim Village – ranger programs. (2023, August 12). National Park Service. https://www.nps.gov/grca/planyourvisit/sr-programs.htm

Special use permits. (2023, February 7). National Park Service. https://www.nps.gov/yell/planyourvisit/special-use-permits.htm

Sprague Lake Loop. (2023, August 21). National Park Service. https://www.nps.gov/thingstodo/romo_spraguelake.htm

Stay and play all year round. (n.d.). Spirit Lake Lodge. https://www.spiritlakelodge.com/

Stay at the Grand Canyon Lodge at North Rim. (2023, May 19). My Grand Canyon Park. https://www.mygrandcanyonpark.com/where-to-stay-camp-eat/hotels-cabins/inside-the-park/grand-canyon-lodge-north-rim/

Steve. (2021, February 1). *10 best stargazing spots in Yosemite and Madera County.* Yosemite This Year. https://www.yosemitethisyear.com/10-best-stargazing-spots-in-yosemite-and-madera-county

Suggested hikes. (2020, November 13). National Park Service. https://www.nps.gov/romo/planyourvisit/hikes.htm

Sunrise. (2023). US News. https://travel.usnews.com/Mount_Rainier_National_Park_WA/Things_To_Do/Sunrise_63874/

The Ahwahnee. (2023). Travel Yosemite. https://www.travelyosemite.com/lodging/the-ahwahnee/

The history of Yosemite National Park. (2023). National Park Reservations. https://www.nationalparkreservations.com/article/yosemite-the-history-of-yosemite-national-park/#:~:text=Yosemite%20Valley%20was%20home%20to,the%20naming%20of%20Yosemite%20Valley.

Things to do. (2023, July 24). National Park Service. https://www.nps.gov/grca/planyourvisit/things2do.htm

Thomas, L. (2023). *6 Grand Canyon hiking trails that will take your breath away.* 57 Hours. https://57hours.com/best-of/grand-canyon-hiking/

Thunderbird Lodge. (2015, November 19). My Grand Canyon Park. https://www.mygrandcanyonpark.com/where-to-stay-camp-eat/hotels-cabins/inside-the-park/thunderbird-lodge/

Tim. (2023, June 22). *Grand Canyon helicopter tour: Everything you need to know.* Earth Trekkers. https://www.earthtrekkers.com/grand-canyon-helicopter-tour-everything-you-need-to-know/

Top things to see and do in Grand Teton National Park. (2022). Jackson Hole WY. https://www.jacksonholewy.com/blog/top-things-to-see-do-in-grand-teton-national-park/

Trail Ridge Road scenic drive in Rocky Mountain National Park. (n.d.). Rocky Mountain National Park. https://www.rockymountainnationalpark.com/gallery/drive-trr/

Tuolumne Meadows Lodge. (2023). Travel Yosemite. https://www.travelyosemite.com/lodging/tuolumne-meadows-lodge/

20 minutes from the Grand Canyon. (n.d.). Grand Canyon Inn. https://grandcanyoninn.com/index.html

Visitor Centers. (2022, January 25). National Park Service. https://www.nps.gov/yell/planyourvisit/visitorcenters.htm

Visitor centers. (n.d.). All Yosemite. https://www.allyosemite.com/park_info/visitor_centers.php

Watch wildlife. (2021, May 18). National Park Service. https://www.nps.gov/yell/planyourvisit/viewanim.htm

Wawona Hotel. (2023). Travel Yosemite. https://www.travelyosemite.com/lodging/wawona-hotel/

Welcome to Hotel Estes. (n.d.). Hotel Estes. https://www.hotelestes.com/

Western Riviera Lakeside Lodging. (n.d.). Wester Riviera. https://www.westernriv.com/

What are the typical seasons and road closures in Yellowstone? (n.d.). Yellowstone Park Net. https://www.yellowstoneparknet.com/park_info/hours_seaso ns.php#:~:text=What%20are%20the%20typical%20seasons,ye ar%2C%2024%20hours%20a%20day.

Where mountains of memories are made. (n.d.). Grand Lake Lodge. https://www.grandlakelodge.com/

Why is Yellowstone called Yellowstone? (2023). USGS. https://www.usgs.gov/faqs/why-yellowstone-called-yellowstone#:~:text=Instead%2C%20the%20name%20was%2 0attributed,and%20northeast%20of%20the%20Park.

Wildlife viewing. (2022, December 8). National Park Service. https://www.nps.gov/grte/planyourvisit/wildview.htm

Wildlife viewing. (2023, August). Visit Rainier. https://visitrainier.com/wildlife-viewing/#:~:text=At%20Mount%20Rainier%20National%20Park,be%20spotted%20in%20forested%20habitats

Winter activities. (2023, April 16). National Park Service. https://www.nps.gov/yose/planyourvisit/wintersports.htm

Winter backcountry camping. (2022, December 15). National Park Service. https://www.nps.gov/yell/planyourvisit/winter-backcountry-camping.htm

Winter recreation. (2023, May 30). National Park Service. https://www.nps.gov/mora/planyourvisit/winter-recreation.htm

World famous mule rides. (n.d.). Grand Canyon Lodges. https://www.grandcanyonlodges.com/plan/mule-rides/

Yavapai Museum of Geology. (2023, March 5). National Park Service. https://www.nps.gov/grca/planyourvisit/yavapai-geo.htm

Yellowstone at 150 years. (2023). Yellowstone Forever. https://www.yellowstone.org/yellowstone150/#:~:text=History%20of%20Yellowstone,Grant.

Yellowstone National Park operating hours and seasons. (2022). National Parks. https://www.inationalparks.com/national-parks/yellowstone-national-park/yellowstone-national-park-information/yellowstone-national-park-operating-hours-seasons/

Yosemite fees & passes. (2023, May 15). National Park Service. https://www.nps.gov/yose/planyourvisit/fees.htm

Yosemite operating hours and seasons. (2023, May 16). National Park Service. https://www.nps.gov/yose/planyourvisit/hours.htm#:~:text=

Yosemite%20National%20Park%20is%20open,conditions%20
and%20Hetch%20Hetchy%20hours

Yosemite Park history, timeline, and evolution. (2023). Scenic Wonders.
https://www.scenicwonders.com/yosemite-park-history

Yosemite Park stargazing. (2018, November 22). Scenic Wonders.
https://www.scenicwonders.com/yosemite-park-
attractions/yosemite-stargazing

Yosemite permits & reservations. (2023, February 27). National Park
Service.
https://www.nps.gov/yose/planyourvisit/permitsandreservati
ons.htm

Yosemite Valley day hikes. (2022, April 6). National Park Service.
https://www.nps.gov/yose/planyourvisit/valleyhikes.htm

Yosemite Valley Lodge. (2023). Travel Yosemite.
https://www.travelyosemite.com/lodging/yosemite-valley-
lodge/

Yosemite Valley Loop Trail. (2022, May 19). National Park Service.
https://www.nps.gov/yose/planyourvisit/valleylooptrail.htm

Yosemite Valley. (2022, June 2). National Park Service.
https://www.nps.gov/yose/planyourvisit/yv.htm

Zelazko, A. (2023, August 16). *Rocky Mountain National Park.*
Britannica. https://www.britannica.com/place/Rocky-
Mountain-National-Park